D1571129

The Spiritual Guide

The Spiritual Guide

Four Steps on the Path of Enlightenment

RICHARD WHITE

CASCADE *Books* · Eugene, Oregon

THE SPIRITUAL GUIDE
Four Steps on the Path of Enlightenment

Cascade Books
An Imprint of Wipf and Stock Publishers
199 W. 8th Ave., Suite 3
Eugene, OR 97401

www.wipfandstock.com

PAPERBACK ISBN: 978-1-4982-9483-6
HARDBACK ISBN: 978-1-4982-9485-0
EBOOK ISBN: 978-1-4982-9484-3

Cataloging-in-Publication data:

Names: White, Richard J. (Richard John), 1956–.

Title: The spiritual guide : four steps on the path of enlightenment / Richard White.

Description: Eugene, OR: Cascade Books | Includes bibliographical references and index.

Identifiers: ISBN: 978-1-4982-9483-6 (paperback) | 978-1-4982-9485-0 (hardback) | 978-1-4982-9484-3 (ebook)

Subjects: LCSH: Spiritual life. | Spirituality.

Classification: BL624 W465 2016 (print) | BL624 (ebook)

Manufactured in the U.S.A.   NOVEMBER 8, 2016

For Clarinda
With love and gratitude

Contents

Preface

THIS BOOK IS A guide to spirituality and what it means to live a spiritual life. The basic question is, how can I live a more genuine life—a life that can lead to enlightenment? There are many responses to this question, and several competing claims. But there is also some agreement between different philosophical and religious views on what it means to be spiritually centered. As a professional philosopher, I have been blessed with the time to think about ultimate questions, and I have been able to study different spiritual traditions in depth. But spiritual writings are often difficult, and "spirituality" is an elusive theme. How are we to make sense of it all? I wanted to think these things through; and so, with some trepidation, I began to outline a very simple account of what it means to live in a spiritual way. My goal was to write a book that would appeal to intelligent readers who had the passion as well as the courage to come to grips with spiritual matters—people who take such things seriously and who are willing to change their lives if they need to. *The Spiritual Guide: Four Steps on the Path of Enlightenment* is the book that I wanted to write. And while it is a short book, it is also the outcome of spiritual and intellectual striving that aims at the heart of wisdom itself.

This book does not support any specific doctrines, and it has something to say to all people, regardless of their religious affiliation or lack of it. I do not assume anything about the nature of God or the self, the reality of karma, reincarnation, or personal immortality. All of these ideas are quite independent of the spiritual framework that I argue for here. But like everyone else, I do have my own perspective: My great-grandfather was a Methodist minister preaching hellfire and damnation; I was brought up in England in the Anglican church; I have taught for some time at a Jesuit Catholic university in the United States; and I have studied different world philosophies; I am also drawn to contemporary spiritual writings, and I have spent some time with alternative healing arts and meditation. But I have not written this book as an apologist for any particular religion; and in spite of my own philosophical background, I am not a Platonist, a Daoist, an Aristotelian or a Stoic. I believe that there is some spiritual truth in all of these approaches and this is the reason for their enduring appeal. I have also come to think that there is a basic wisdom in the world that is applicable to all human beings, regardless of where they come from or at what point in time they happen to live. Spiritual wisdom can be found in many places, and we only have to look for it—not only in religion, philosophy, and art, but also in everyday life, and the people who are all around us. Wisdom or enlightenment is definitely not a *private* possession, and no one has a monopoly of spiritual truth.

This book should speak to anyone who is interested in spiritual matters: Seekers and skeptics; students and students of life; philosophers, atheists, agnostics, and defenders of the faith. "Information," or the state of our knowledge, is forever changing from one day to the next; and in the modern age, we are frequently distracted or even addicted to whatever the new technology brings us. But the nature of spiritual wisdom remains constant over time, and it is available to all of us. In this book, I sketch out four of the most important aspects of spiritual understanding, or the four steps on the path of enlightenment. Taken together, I think they represent the most basic spiritual themes and the true focus of a spiritual life. I hope this will resonate with your own view of things, and help you to think more clearly about matters of ultimate concern.

1

Spirituality

WHEN I WAS A student, I fell in love with philosophy. Philosophy can help you to think more critically and more thoughtfully about the world; but more than anything else, philosophy seems to ask all the big questions: What is the meaning of life? What does it mean to live a good life? Does God exist? And how can I be true to myself? Philosophy is literally the love of wisdom, and the true philosopher is a *lover* of wisdom. Not a guru figure who claims to have all the answers but a seeker who longs to discover the truth about things, like the lover who yearns for the one that he loves.

Now I am a professional philosopher, but in recent years I have become more involved in the field of spirituality, which is, I think, the very heart of wisdom itself. I have studied classical texts as well as New Age writings. I have become more familiar with spiritual practices, and I teach classes in "World Philosophy" and "The Philosophy of Spiritual Life," which looks at important spiritual themes such as compassion, forgiveness, reverence, and the sacred. I am not surprised that my students are anxious to talk about spiritual questions and matters of ultimate concern. In today's world, there is so much pressure to compete for a career or just to get a job, while the most important issues that everyone has to deal with are neglected or viewed as irrelevant. But the fact is, before you are a nurse or a teacher or a computer programmer, you are a human being; and as a human being you must set out on your own path to think about ultimate meaning, values, and truth, all of which are key to living a spiritual life. This is not always an easy path, and it is very easy to get distracted; but as Socrates famously said: "the unexamined life is not worth living."

For the most part, philosophers use reason and argument to get to the truth of things. And *philosophy* can be a very critical enterprise that calls established truths into question, not just for the sake of being skeptical or perverse, but to see which of our ideas *can* be justified, and which are based on something like "faith" alone. *Spirituality* on the other hand is much more intuitive and it uses basic insights about human life to describe how we are meant to live and fulfill the most serious part of ourselves. Of course, spirituality is not the same thing as *religion*. Some people believe in God, but their lives seem to be largely unaffected by this belief, which is just an *intellectual* commitment. Other people, including some atheists and agnostics, are drawn to living the most spiritual and meaningful lives possible but they cannot make a faith commitment or accept the idea of personal immortality. At this point, even after some years of practice and philosophical study, I don't have a simple, straightforward definition of what "spirituality" is; but as a useful way to begin this book, I will argue that spirituality can be thought about in at least three different ways—and this brings me now to the core of my own ideas about this subject.

The Nature of Spirituality

First of all, I think that a spiritual life is the opposite of what we would call a materialistic life, which is devoted to the pursuit of wealth, prestige, or power over others. The selfish and unspiritual life is self-involved and unconcerned with matters of ultimate significance. At the same time, however, a spiritual life is not just a life that is focused on "otherworldly" matters. More than anything else, living a spiritual life means recognizing the true meaning and value of *this* life, trying to live authentically in the world, and keeping more selfish concerns in their proper perspective. In many spiritual traditions, the ultimate goal is to overcome the ordinary and petty concerns of the ego and to embrace the deeper reality where everything is connected and one. In Christianity, for example, the goal is to identify one's own will with the will of God, and to lose oneself by surrendering to God's will. In Hindu Vedanta philosophy, we are told to reject the standpoint of the separate individual—which is an illusion—and to embrace the ultimate undivided reality of "Brahman," for "That art thou!"[1] In Buddhism, the cultivation of compassion inspires a sense of interconnectedness—which includes the value of *all* sentient life—and this is held to be the deepest

1. From "The Chandogya Upanishad," in *The Upanishads*, 185.

wisdom of all. From this kind of perspective, individuality is an illusion, or at least a very limited point of view, which is fostered by selfish concerns. And it typically leads to alienation as we sense our separation from nature, from other people, and the community we belong to. So the spiritual remedy for this is to overcome "materialism" and the *false* perspective of the individual self. In this respect, we can think of spirituality as a movement away from materialism and the ordinary values of commercial society that we usually find so powerful and absorbing.

Second, this means that a spiritual life must involve a *quest* or a journey in search of ultimate truth. It is a life lived in terms of questions: How should I live? What should I believe? What is the purpose of my life? And such a life is absolutely committed to making progress in becoming a better person, or one who is more fulfilled and well-adjusted to existence itself. Many people experience alienation in the sense of not feeling at home in the world or with others. But I think a truly spiritual person can achieve a sense of belonging, which means that he or she must be prepared to *trust* in life; and in spite of the problems, and even the tragedies that life throws out to most of us, he or she will remain committed to the idea that life is basically a good thing. Over the course of history, many important spiritual paths have been established, including Christianity, Platonism, Buddhism, Stoicism, Confucianism, and others. Some people seek union with God; others search for nirvana or the Absolute or the *Dao*, which is "the way." In ancient Vedanta philosophy, the three paths of *karma yoga, bhakti yoga,* and *jnani yoga* correspond to the way of work, the way of religious devotion, and the way of study and meditation respectively.

Today, we live in a global society where *all* of these different paths can be studied, while at the same time we are not always so bound to the traditions and ideas that we have inherited from the past. This means that spiritual life is likely to involve more active discernment on the part of each individual seeker, where the point is to dialogue with different spiritual perspectives in order to find the truth that is most inspiring in one's own life. And this is important, even as a way of understanding the spiritual tradition that we grew up with, by looking at it with new eyes and from a more global point of view. Today, different spiritual traditions are available to spiritual seekers through the Internet, workshops, books, and classes. This does not mean that spirituality has been diluted, but it is much easier than ever before to come to grips with different paths to determine how

[handwritten margin note: Spirituality not about the individual?]

they speak to us. One thing that hasn't changed is that the spiritual life is a quest or a journey towards the highest truth.

The third point is that spirituality involves becoming aware of the deepest level of life, or what we could also call *ultimate reality and meaning*. This is not to be discovered in e-mails, texts, or idle conversations, for all these things distract us from more important concerns. I am referring to the deeper truth of human existence that we are sometimes able to glimpse in exceptional experiences. When we come close to death, for example, or experience the wonders of nature, or love, we sometimes feel as if all of our ordinary, everyday concerns have been pushed aside, and we can experience the world as it really is. Then we know that we have touched the deepest truth and we have somehow grasped the meaning of life. Of course, we cannot abandon our reason in this spiritual journey, for then we would only believe what we wanted to believe, and our spiritual life would be nothing but wish fulfillment. Philosophy and critical thinking are important because our spiritual ideas and practices must make sense. But the spiritual pursuit is basically a matter of *experience* rather than rational thinking: We recognize and honor spiritual truth as the truth that can be lived; it is the set of values that enhances life instead of diminishing it; and it is the basic standpoint that informs an authentic life.

Four Steps on the Path of Enlightenment

I have written this book on the basis of my teaching, my scholarly work, and my own life experience, and I think that I have something to offer as a fellow-seeker. I have been able to devote myself to fundamental questions of human life, and I have helped others to think about matters of ultimate concern and meaning. I have written about some of these ideas in different scholarly books and essays, but in recent years I have become concerned that academia (and especially academic philosophy) is a closed community. It certainly does not speak to all intelligent readers, many of whom lack philosophical training only because they have chosen to devote their lives to other things. I have written elsewhere about the *arguments* of the philosophers, but in this book I am more interested in the *wisdom* of individuals like Socrates, Buddha, and Jesus. In each case, these teachers sought to inspire people, not just by giving the best arguments—for any argument can be disputed—but by revealing profound truths about the human condition that we can usually recognize for ourselves once they have been pointed out to us. The goal of this short book is to clarify the four most important steps to a spiritually fulfilled life—or the way to enlighten-ment—which can be meditated on and returned to over and over again. For in this way, such important ideas can be taken down and integrated at a deeper level in one's life. Sometimes, as the saying goes, "less is more," and in this book I hope to offer a clear, succinct outline of spirituality that can serve as a framework for future understanding and spiritual growth.

So what are the four steps to enlightenment, or the most important points of spirituality as I understand it here? First, I believe that spiritual life begins with suffering. As long as things are going well for us, we really don't think about the big questions—How should I live? Why am I here?—but when something goes wrong and we experience personal disappoint-ment, pain, despair, or even the death of a loved one, we try to make sense of our lives. We are full of anguish because we have been diagnosed with a terminal illness. Or we suffer the nightmares associated with post-trau-matic stress. We hate ourselves for something we did years ago. In many ways, suffering is the bottom line of human experience. But what is the *right* response to suffering, whether this is our own suffering or somebody else's? Some people say we should be strong and just try to tough it out. In many cultures, including our own, "softness" and sadness are sometimes considered to be signs of weakness because they mean letting our emo-tions rule us instead of rational principles. In the ancient world, the Stoic philosophers said we should cultivate indifference to whatever happens so that we can never be affected by the ups and downs of fortune. And even today, many people believe that whatever happens must be good because God would not allow bad things to happen to good people. So suffering is supposed to be a "test," or a blessing in disguise, and whatever heartbreak or physical and mental anguish people experience is ultimately justified. I have called this chapter "Staying Open to Suffering," because I want to show how all of these responses are ways of avoiding suffering and not dealing with it properly. On the other hand, compassion is the best response to suffering—by which I mean it is the most spiritual response—because it opens up the world to us, instead of shutting us down. And this includes both compassion for the suffering of others and compassion for ourselves, without which we would remain spiritually isolated and in despair.

The second step takes us from compassion to giving and forgiving, which are fundamental forms of generosity. In my view, generosity reflects the exuberance of life itself. As everyone knows, generosity is a moral virtue, for we should share what we have with others and try to avoid being miserly or mean. But in addition to this, we can affirm generosity as a *spiritual* virtue that mirrors the absolute generosity of life. Generosity is always exceptional, for there is no moral requirement or *duty* to be generous; and when we act generously we always go beyond whatever is expected of us. We can give our money and our property to whoever needs these things. But we also act with a generous spirit whenever we give other people our time and our attention, or stay available for whenever they need us. Some people are willing to sacrifice their lives for other people—like Harriet Tubman, who escaped from slavery and risked her own life many times over to help other slaves escape, even though she didn't know them; or like Martin Luther King Jr., who understood that he probably would be killed for demanding civil rights. For many of us, however, the most obvious example of spiritual generosity is forgiveness: We have been unfairly or unjustly treated by someone else, but instead of seeking revenge or restitution, we decide to renounce all of our claims upon the offender. We forgive him—and this act of spiritual generosity allows both of us to get on with our lives. *Living a generous life* reflects the generosity of life, and it means we are in fundamental accord with the goodness of the world.

Following compassion and generosity, the third step is about cultivating mindfulness and wonder. Today we spend so much time separated from the world around us. We are plugged into computers and other devices and as a result we don't cherish nature, and we are unable to value the experience of anything that is greater than we are—including art, truth, music, and scholarship, and, many would also say, *God*. The world has become flat, wisdom has been reduced to information, and there is nothing apart from the "facts." In this context, it is absolutely necessary to cultivate a sense of wonder through different experiences that allow us to recover the *sacred* character of the world. For the sacred is not an "otherworldly" place and it can be experienced in the very life we are living now. But this can only happen by living fully in the present, and by living completely at every single moment. We cannot live in regret, focusing on the past that is over and done with, and we cannot use the present as just a stepping-stone to the future—for in either case we devalue the reality of the present. Some poets and philosophers have written about the inspiration of beauty, while artists have sought to show the beauty of the natural world. Other writers have talked about the "sublime" or the grandeur of nature, which we encounter whenever we contemplate the starry sky at night, magnificent mountains, or even a storm at sea. Such experiences can be overwhelming, but at the same time they are also uplifting, and they put us back in touch with the natural world that we belong to. The world is held to contain many extraordinary miracles and wonders, including the kinds of miracles that are described in the Bible and other sacred texts. But it also contains many *ordinary* miracles of kindness, beauty, and love; and we should be mindful of all these things because they enhance our spiritual understanding. In the different wisdom traditions, spiritual practices like prayer, meditation, and daily reflection have been developed as ways of cultivating mindfulness and openness to wonder.

Finally, I have called the fourth step, "Accepting Death and Returning to Joy." Some people think that death takes away the meaning of our lives. It seems that we spend our lives creating a world for ourselves: we read books and we study different things, we enjoy relationships with others, and through challenging experiences we learn who we really are. In this way, we can grow both ethically and spiritually. But then it all ends in death, and this doesn't make sense because it seems as if it was all for nothing. What is the point of life if it ends with the grave? And even if we consider ourselves to be safe for the time being, we can still be shattered by the death of those we love. Perhaps we can maintain a good attitude towards life if we focus on heavenly rewards—but then we may start to devalue this life by thinking of it as just a path to the next life, and this would show ingratitude for what we have been given now. In the final chapter, I want to think about how we can cultivate an authentic and reasonable attitude toward death, while staying open to the possibility of joy in this life—for there really isn't much point in living if we decide that death makes life meaningless and absurd! Here I will show how philosophy, or critical reflection on ultimate issues, can help us to achieve this standpoint. And in this regard, it should become clear that philosophy is itself a kind of spiritual practice.

Many of the ancient philosophers—the Stoics, early Buddhist thinkers, and others—used memory techniques and different kinds of thought experiments to keep themselves focused on the goals of spiritual life. Such practices include setting intentions at the beginning of each day, and examining oneself at the end of the day; meditation on important themes, and prayer. In this book, I will discuss all of these practices, but I will also focus attention on spiritual questions by using parables, stories, and other writings that provide a powerful account of wisdom. These stories come from a variety of different wisdom traditions—Buddhist and Christian,

Daoist and Islamic, Socratic and Stoic to name but some among many. Thinking about generosity and love is important, but the story of the Good Samaritan encapsulates many of these ideas, and points us in the right spiritual direction. Likewise, the problem of suffering is a huge topic, but the story of Job (in Judaism) or Kisagotami (in Buddhism) shows how suffering can lead to empathy and connection with others. And in this way, it might be possible to consider whether suffering is a part of the meaning of life. Parables and stories often contain the deepest spiritual truths about human beings. Of course, they never come with supporting arguments or "proofs"—but the whole point of such stories is that the reader or the listener has to do some work to understand what the story is really all about. Take the parable of the Good Samaritan or the parable of the Prodigal Son. These stories are about true compassion and forgiveness, and they give us an inspiring model for our ethical and spiritual life. Through reflection and thinking things through, we can make these stories our own, and we can incorporate their truth at the deepest level of who we are. But even if we don't completely understand a parable or a story when we first hear it, there is usually a shock of recognition because the story rings true, and we realize that the author—if there ever *was* an original author—must have been a wise person who knew what life was all about.

Plato and the Story of the Cave

To bring some of these basic ideas together, I want to turn to the story of the Cave, which appears at the high point of Plato's masterpiece, the *Republic*. The *Republic* is one of the most important works of philosophy ever written, and it is certainly the most influential. Like many of Plato's works, it unfolds as a dialogue between Socrates and others. In the *Republic*, Plato offers a significant account of the nature of justice, and he constructs a model of the ideal city in speech: What does the perfectly just society look like? But the *Republic* is also a discussion of knowledge and the different levels of reality that exist; and in the story of the Cave, Plato gives us a parable concerning the true nature of the human condition. I teach this passage in all of my beginning philosophy classes because it seems to say something about the nature of philosophy, and what it means to be a true philosopher. But at the same time, it also gives us the picture of a spiritual quest in which someone leaves the comfort of the cave and ventures out into the higher and more challenging realms of spiritual life.

The story of the Cave comes out of a dialogue between Socrates and his friend Glaucon. This is how Plato begins his story:

> And now, I said, let me show in a figure how far our nature is enlightened or unenlightened:—Behold! human beings living in an underground den, which has a mouth open towards the light and reaching all along the den; here they have been from their childhood, and have their legs and necks chained so that they cannot move, and can only see before them, being prevented by the chains from turning round their heads. Above and behind them a fire is blazing at a distance, and between the fire and the prisoners there is a raised way; and you will see, if you look, a low wall built along the way, like the screen which marionette players have in front of them, over which they show the puppets.
>
> I see.
>
> And do you see, I said, men passing along the wall carrying all sorts of vessels, and statues and figures of animals made of wood and stone and various materials, which appear over the wall? Some of them are talking, others silent.
>
> You have shown me a strange image, and they are strange prisoners.
>
> Like ourselves, I replied; and they see only their own shadows, or the shadows of one another, which the fire throws on the opposite wall of the cave?
>
> True, he said; how could they see anything but the shadows if they were never allowed to move their heads?
>
> And of the objects which are being carried in like manner they would only see the shadows?
>
> Yes, he said.[2]

I think the cave (or "den") represents our ordinary, everyday life. For the most part we find ourselves bound down by all of our chains—which are the prejudices and received ideas that we have inherited from society—and we are forced to look straight ahead at what is immediately in front of us on the wall of the cave itself. But the shadows that preoccupy us are by no means the most important things. True, they are supposed to be the desirable objects of the society we belong to, and they would include all the trappings of wealth, power, popularity and fame: a new car, a better job, perhaps a television appearance, and so on. But these are only the *shadows* of things that are truly important or real. Then, Plato says that one man manages to escape from his chains. In fact, he is *forced* into the light:

2. Plato, *Republic* 514a–515b.

And suppose once more, that he is reluctantly dragged up a steep and rugged ascent, and held fast until he's forced into the presence of the sun himself, is he not likely to be pained and irritated? When he approaches the light his eyes will be dazzled, and he will not be able to see anything at all of what are now called realities.

Not all in a moment, he said.

He will require to grow accustomed to the sight of the upper world. And first he will see the shadows best, next the reflections of men and other objects in the water, and then the objects themselves; then he will gaze upon the light of the moon and the stars and the spangled heaven; and he will see the sky and the stars by night better than the sun or the light of the sun by day?

Certainly.

Last of all he will be able to see the sun, and not mere reflections of it in the water, but he will see it in its own proper place, and not in another; and he will contemplate it as it is.[3]

All of which gives us the sense that there are different levels of reality and understanding. Most people will remain in the cave and be totally absorbed and preoccupied by what is immediately in front of them. They will always be obsessed by prestige, power, or money. But it is possible to move closer to the fire and ultimately to escape from the cave altogether, to contemplate the sun, which symbolizes the highest reality of all.

Now, one thing that Plato seems to be saying in this story is that every spiritual quest or journey has at least two parts: First, we have to escape from the chains of everyday life, the prejudices of our culture and our upbringing, as we make our way towards the sun, which is the source of all being and the highest reality of all. In Plato's parable, the sun is the symbol of the absolute, which he identifies elsewhere as "the Good," and this is the goal of spiritual enlightenment. But once we reach this ultimate point, we will also feel compelled to share our vision with others. And this makes sense: The spiritual quest is not a selfish pursuit where the goal is nothing more than individual fulfillment or even personal enlightenment. And when we are spiritually accomplished, we are bound to return to the cave to inspire others with what we have learned. Presumably, this is why all the great wisdom figures, including Socrates, Buddha, Confucius, and Jesus, were also *teachers*, because they wanted others to experience the same enlightenment they had experienced for themselves.

3. Ibid., 515e–516c.

In another parable, the famous "Oxherding Tale" in Zen Buddhism, the search for the ox is another metaphor of the quest for enlightenment. In this story, which is usually told in ten different pictures, we begin by finding traces of "the ox." Then we catch the ox, we learn how to control it, and, eventually, when we reach home, the ox is forgotten because the spiritual goal has been accomplished and we are living a spiritual life: "Whip, tether, self, and ox all have merged, no traces remain . . . Having reached home, you are in accord with the ancient way."[4] But once again, the achievement of enlightenment is followed by the return to the human community: "Entering the marketplace barefoot and unadorned. Blissfully smiling, though covered with dust and ragged of clothes. Using no supernatural power, you bring the withered trees spontaneously into bloom."[5] Now our insights are to be put to the test as they are communicated to others. And we can embody the pure generosity of life by inspiring others with the same urgent desire for spiritual awakening as a task that must be undertaken *now*.

But returning to the cave of ignorance can be dangerous. Some people just don't understand why anyone would prefer spiritual truth to everyday success, and they would even deny that there is such a thing as "spiritual wisdom"—especially in our own information age when all the truth in the world is supposedly available on the Internet. The one who returns to the cave is ridiculed by those who have remained behind. He tries to communicate his spiritual understanding to them, but in the story that Plato tells, they just laugh at him, and they would even do violence to him if they could: "And if anyone tried to loose another and lead him up to the light, let them only catch the offender, and they would put him to death."[6] In this passage, of course, Plato is telling us the story of Socrates, but it is also the story of many other wisdom figures, such as Jesus, Gandhi, or Martin Luther King Jr., who devoted their lives to bringing truth to others. Clearly, the possession of wisdom is not an unmixed blessing, for the world is not always ready for those who have the deepest understanding of spiritual matters and truth. And death can be the reward for enlightenment.

As we have noted, Plato's story of the Cave is a parable about philosophy. It discusses the nature of philosophy as a kind of turning away from whatever is here and now to grasp the deeper reality that underlies the world and makes it what it is. But at the same time, it is also a parable about

---

4. I have used the translation by Loori in *Riding the Ox Home*, 55.

5. Ibid., 67.

6. Plato, *Republic* 517a.

the authentic spiritual quest—against materialism, towards reality and truth, and back into everyday life again. It does not involve the rejection of this life as something secondary and unimportant, and it does not advocate escapism. Instead, it tells us that we should free ourselves from the chains of convention to make our journey towards ultimate reality and truth; but when we are spiritually accomplished, we are bound to communicate our vision to others.

Criticizing Spirituality

All of which brings us to an important point. Some people are disdainful of spirituality and "spiritual issues" because they believe that spirituality is a kind of escapism from the challenges of contemporary life. It is nice to be enlightened, they say, but what about the terrible problems that face the world today, which seem to threaten the well-being of billions of people, as well as future generations who have not even been born yet? From an environmental standpoint, there is pollution and species extinction, climate change, the destruction of the rain forest, and growing rates of cancer among children. From a social and political standpoint, there is the continual threat of nuclear war, terrorism, and state-sponsored violence. And there is a great inequality of wealth between, on the one hand, a handful of billionaires and, on the other hand, billions who have absolutely nothing. All of these things—disease, war, violence, and poverty—seriously undermine the possibility of living a good life, and they undermine the basic conditions for spiritual flourishing and growth. Karl Marx famously said that "religion is the opium of the people"—by which he meant that religion is a distraction from real life, since it allows us to put up with things that should be intolerable. Today some critics would say that "spirituality" is also a kind of avoidance strategy; for when we focus on our own enlightenment and spiritual fulfillment, we are not dealing with the troubles of the real world, but living in a selfish way.

So there are two very different points of view here, and it may be impossible to reconcile them: For the spiritual seeker, political activists are far too angry and aggressive about all the injustice in the world. Of course, no one can deny that there is a lot of unfairness, injustice, and even evil in the world today. But to *hate* injustice and those who perpetrate injustice, and to be *angry* about oppression, pollution, and poverty is just to contribute to a negative spiral that will never accomplish anything that is lasting or

anger can lead to positives though

good. Anger only leads to more anger; just as violence only leads to more violence. The Russian revolution against the privileged ruling class only led to more repression, and the death of millions of people in the long run. War and terrorism usually lead to more war and terrorism; and there is no "war to end all wars," apart from the war that may eventually destroy all of humankind. Unless we change the world from within—which means starting with ourselves—human life will always involve hostility and conflict. As Gandhi is supposed to have said, "You should be the change that you want to see in the world."[7] But without an enlightened spiritual attitude, which includes compassion, forgiveness and love, the world will never change, and the old values will remain even if different people are in charge.

For the social or political activist, on the other hand, spiritual concerns appear to sidestep reality. Social and political problems require real-life solutions. And given the state of the world today, encouraging *spiritual* striving seems to be a pointless waste of time. How do compassion, forgiveness, and love really change anything in this world for the better? Those who really live by these values can be exploited and are easily dealt with because they are usually unwilling to fight back. They have "beautiful souls," but they are useless because they don't want to get their hands dirty; and they seem to be more concerned with their own spiritual progress than the fate of the world and all the people in it. Those who are involved in social and political struggles can also point out that "spirituality" has become big business. Like everything else, "spirituality" is now a commodity to be bought and sold, with expensive seminars and retreats, motivational tapes and CDs, books (like this one?), and spiritual paraphernalia. Well-known spiritual masters charge exorbitant fees for their classes or lectures; but why should spiritual wisdom have to cost so much? And what does it mean that so many spiritual leaders are incredibly wealthy and famous? All of which suggests that spirituality is harmless at best; but it is also a part of the problem if it makes us oblivious to social transformation and the real needs of others.

The two examples that I used earlier—Plato's story of the Cave and the Oxherding Tale—imply, at first, that spiritual development is a purely individual matter that has nothing to do with others or the society at large. It is up to each one of us to decide whether we really want to leave the cave of ignorance or track down the bull of enlightenment; no one is going to

---

7. This is usually attributed to Gandhi, but it may be a summary of his position rather than a direct quote.

strike all our chains off and lead us into the light, and this is something that we have to do for ourselves. But remember, the second part of the spiritual quest involves an encounter with others, and an attempt to show them—through teaching or just by being there and making a difference in their lives—that spiritual enlightenment is possible and even *necessary* in some sense. In the end, spirituality and politics do not have to be conflicting forces, and there are plenty of cases where a spiritually enlightened individual has a very realistic understanding of how the world works, so that he or she can help to change the world for the better.

Mahatma Gandhi, Martin Luther King Jr., Aung San Suu Kyi, and Dorothy Day are just a few of the spiritual individuals who have led movements for social justice and equality. And they used their spiritual understanding and their political savvy—their courage and their wisdom—to make real progress in improving the world, leaving it a better place for people to live in. Likewise, the contemporary environmental movement is both political and profoundly spiritual in nature. Those who support efforts to reduce pollution and clean up rivers usually have a very strong spiritual interest in the beauty and the inherent value of the natural world that is under threat; they feel a commitment to future generations who should be allowed to appreciate and enjoy these things like we do; but at the same time, they are often quite pragmatic in their political involvements. The civil rights movement was inspired by Christians and pacifists, and it continues to be so. In recent years, different forms of engaged Buddhism have also emerged, because compassion, which is the fundamental value in Buddhism, involves a commitment to others and a desire to reduce suffering in every possible way.

Thus, in different ways, spiritual transformation and the transformation of the world are linked together, and the two are by no means opposed to each other. We often think of spirituality as a purely individual achievement, but at the same time, many social movements, including environmentalism, the peace movement, and the civil rights movement, are spiritually inspired, and this has made them more effective in the long run. Today we have a greater sense than ever before that we belong to a *global* community, where the rights of other people are important to us, even if they live on the other side of the world. We even care about future generations of people who are still unborn, but who will inherit this world after we are gone. In this book, I focus on spirituality as a journey towards ultimate truth and enlightenment. But it should be clear by now that spirituality, like religion, belongs to the individual and to the community itself. All the criticisms of spirituality must be taken seriously, but there is a deeper wisdom that lies beyond or beneath our everyday understanding of things; and I think it is possible to discover this *spiritual* reality, though not without some difficulty or the willingness to risk ourselves.

There is a lot of suffering in the world today. Many people live lives that are cut short by terrorism and war; and many more suffer from poverty, disease, and malnutrition. Against this background, a "spiritual" life sometimes seems like an irrelevant luxury. Should we just shrug our shoulders and say that life is unfair? Or perhaps we can do something about it by living a more mindful and generous life that is open to the suffering of others. We must also bear in mind that there is a big difference between these two questions: 1) What do we need in order to live? And 2) What is it that makes life worth living? The questions are obviously related to each other, but while we need food, shelter, clean air and water, and peace to survive, mere survival is not enough to make life meaningful and worth living. For this we need to consider the spiritual dimension of life, which can be inspiring, regardless of our ultimate beliefs and commitments.

In this book, I want to offer you some of the most relevant conclusions that I have reached after a long, and ongoing study of philosophy and spiritual life. I want to present these ideas in a straightforward, nontechnical way in order to reach as many different readers as possible. But at the same time, some of these ideas may require more sustained reflection and meditation on the part of readers, just to make them more real. We can know something *intellectually*, but if it does not affect the way that we live, we probably don't know it at all. In addition, there is the issue of spiritual pride: As we have seen, one of the goals of spiritual life is to challenge the priority of the ordinary, selfish ego. But that same ego is quite cunning and it is capable of using anything for its own promotion and benefit, including spirituality itself. For we may be very *proud* of our own spiritual accomplishments, and in this way the spiritual quest may become just another way of feeding our own egoistic self, in opposition to all those others whom we regard as unenlightened. We should beware of such a danger, and in this respect there actually is a spiritual value in failure and disappointment, which return us to the real world and who we really are. In short, we must avoid the heroic model of spiritual success, which reasserts the ego that should be overcome! At the same time, we should not think of spirituality as a kind of escapism or an otherworldly ideal, but as a genuine presence in *this* world, regardless of the next.

There are many different spiritual paths, and in this book I have no interest in arguing for the absolute superiority of any one of them. On the contrary, I think they must all have some validity, especially if they have inspired countless people over an extended period of time. Every kind of spiritual approach offers something different. Our own situation is never the same as anyone else's, and each spiritual approach offers a different kind of "medicine" that may or may not be the right one for us. However, in this book I have tried to clarify what I think are the four essential aspects of any authentic spirituality—and this is not a complicated account. The four steps on the path of enlightenment include openness to suffering, living a generous life, cultivating mindfulness and wonder, and accepting death but affirming joy. And from these four steps we can derive the following spiritual rules: Stay open to suffering! Live a generous life! Cultivate mindfulness and wonder! Accept death and return to joy! By arguing for each of these in turn, I hope to inspire spirituality and cultivate the way to enlightenment. We begin with the problem of suffering.

2

Staying Open to Suffering

WHERE DID THE IMPULSE to critical thinking come from? Why did people start to ask metaphysical questions—about the meaning of life or the existence of God or the nature of ultimate reality? And at what point did people start to question the answers they had been given by traditional authorities, like their rulers or their priests? Plato says that philosophy begins with wonder, and this makes a lot of sense, for if you were never puzzled by the world or astonished by the sheer accident of your own existence, it would never even occur to you to ask, Why is there something rather than nothing? And you would never even wonder why God created the world—if indeed he did—or what is the part that you have to play in the big picture of things. In this respect, philosophy differs from faith. It is not satisfied with stories about God or the gods, and it calls for <u>reasons</u> and <u>arguments</u> to justify our beliefs and our actions. Can we prove the existence of God? Are faith and reason opposites, or can we use our reason to justify our faith? Is there a life after death? Obviously, we cannot answer all of these questions here, but I want to suggest that philosophy and religion do have a common origin in the sense that both of them respond to a basic human need.

But what *is* this basic human need that inspires both reflection and worship? It could be a sense of wonder; it could be the desire to give thanks, or the hope of a life to come. The more I think about it, though, I think the one question that we all have to deal with is the problem of suffering. For at some point in our lives, we will be faced with questions like this: Why is this thing happening to me? What have I done to deserve this? Why do bad things happen to good people? and even, Why do good things happen to people who are bad? This is the problem of suffering, and I think it is at the root of religion and philosophy, and every kind of profound metaphysical inquiry. And in this respect, it is also the origin of our spiritual life.

Let's think about this point. In <u>Buddhism</u>, the problem of suffering is certainly the most fundamental issue. According to legend, Siddhartha Gautama was a prince who lived in a pleasure palace sheltered from all the turmoil of the world. One day he traveled outside of the palace and encountered a sick man, an old man, and finally a dead man. Immediately, he realized that life is problematic because people suffer and die, and he set out on a quest to resolve the problem of suffering. He went from one guru to another and he became an ascetic, a devotee of meditation and other spiritual practices. Eventually, he experienced enlightenment, and as the Buddha he preached the famous fire sermon in which he proclaimed the four noble truths—first, that life is suffering; second, that suffering is caused by attachment—to oneself, to other people, or to things; third, that release from suffering comes by relinquishing attachment; and finally, that *this* is to be accomplished by living in terms of the eightfold path—which includes ethics, different aspects of meditation or mind control, and the true understanding of wisdom.

In Judaism, one of the very oldest sacred texts—possibly the oldest text of the Hebrew Bible—is the book of Job, which is all about the problem of undeserved suffering and whether a good God could possibly allow terrible things to happen to a good person. In what follows, we shall look at the book of Job in more detail because it is a powerful story about this basic issue. In Islam the story of Job is paralleled by the story of Ayyub. Christianity is founded on the image of the suffering Christ on the cross, and Jesus says, "Take up your cross and follow me!"[1]—Which implies that if you become a Christian and live a Christian life, your own suffering will become more meaningful as you share in the suffering of Christ. Christianity makes sense of suffering as a test that we must undergo to see if we are worthy of redemption; and the earliest Christians embraced martyrdom to show their indifference to worldly pleasure and pain.

Likewise, for the earliest philosophers—Socrates, Pythagoras, the Stoics, and Epicurean thinkers—philosophy was a kind of spiritual medicine that relieved the suffering we cause ourselves by not living or thinking well. For all of these ancient thinkers, philosophy was more than just a set of intellectual problems. It was a way of life whose goal was happiness and the avoidance of suffering that forms a part of every human existence. Pain is

1. Matthew 17:24.

18

inevitable, but so much of our suffering is self-caused by the attitudes we adopt to whatever happens to us. We want what we don't have, and we can't hold on to what we have; people leave us and people die. According to the ancient philosophers, the only thing that we can control is how we respond to what happens. And so we must train ourselves to accept the slings and arrows of outrageous fortune as the will of the cosmos itself.[2]

Suffering and the Story of Job

What is the meaning of suffering? Or does suffering even have a meaning? Perhaps we should say that suffering *takes away* meaning because it undermines our goals and it makes them seem completely unimportant. Sometimes pain and suffering can be educational, and so we say that we can learn through the experience of suffering. I think that without suffering we would stay self-absorbed and oblivious to everything except our own desires. But then something happens and we experience physical, emotional, or spiritual trauma, and we find ourselves pushed away from the world that we enjoy. We are pinned down to ourselves and our situation can become unbearable. Illness, betrayal, the death of a friend, rejection—how can we even begin to make sense of such things, especially if we have an underlying feeling that "life is good," which makes us want to go on living? It makes no sense, and even if nothing bad is happening to us now, we will sooner or later become aware of the fundamental uncertainty of human existence, and the reality of impermanence and change. Maybe we can still find some meaning in personal tragedy, but suffering opens up a whole slew of insistent questions concerning the value of life and its ultimate goal. And sometimes we may never be able to recover from what has happened.

This is the situation described in the book of Job, which was most likely written between the sixth and fourth centuries BCE, although it was probably an oral legend before it was ever written down. At the start of the story, we are told that Job is a good man: he is decent, he gives to the poor, and he is thankful for all of his blessings, his family, wealth, and status. God himself holds him up as an example of a truly good and pious person. Then Satan, or the Accusing Angel, argues with God that Job's religious devotion is based entirely on his good fortune. And he claims that this would become self-evident if God were to test Job by making him suffer. But this is the

---

2. See Pierre Hadot's discussion of ancient philosophy in *Philosophy as a Way of Life*.

strangest thing: according to the story, Satan is tempting God, and God succumbs to the temptation by agreeing that he *will* put Job to the test.

First, in an incredible scene, a series of messengers arrive to announce the death of all Job's sons and daughters, and the loss of all his cattle and livestock. Job is distraught, he suffers extreme emotional anguish, but at the end of the day he keeps his faith and his patience: "The LORD gave and the LORD has taken away" he says, "blessed be the name of the LORD."[3] But the test is not over yet, and Job is made to suffer the physical pain of boils all over his body, as well as the spiritual anguish of rejection by God and the rest of the community. Now at last, Job is angry because he knows he has not done anything wrong, and yet he is being punished. Of course, his friends think that he must have been bad, because God is just, and God would never allow anyone to suffer who did not deserve it. As his friend Zophar exclaims with righteous indignation:

> Should a multitude of words go unanswered,
>   and a man full of talk be vindicated?
> Should your babble silence men,
>   and when you mock, shall no one shame you?
> For you say, 'My doctrine is pure,
>   and I am clean in God's eyes.'
> But oh, that God would speak
>   and open his lips to you,
> and that he would tell you the secrets of wisdom!
>   For he is manifold in understanding.
> Know then that God exacts of you less than your guilt deserves.[4]

But Job is insistent—he has not done anything wrong!—and his friends get really scared as he stubbornly proclaims his innocence and demands his day in court with God.

Why would a good and loving God allow bad things to happen to good people? Surely this means that Job is bad, for God would not be good if he allowed such things to occur. Job has no answer to give, but he starts to realize that the sick and the weak can suffer terribly in this life, and his own misery is nothing exceptional—in fact, it is the norm:

3. Job 1:21.
4. Job 11:2–6.

Why are not times of judgment kept by the Almighty,
and why do those who know him never see his days?
Men remove landmarks;
they seize flocks and pasture them.
They drive away the ass of the fatherless;
they take the widow's ox for a pledge.
They thrust the poor off the road;
the poor of the earth all hide themselves.
Behold, like wild asses in the desert
they go forth to their toil,
seeking prey in the wilderness
as food for their children.
They gather their fodder in the field
and they glean the vineyard of the wicked man.
They lie all night naked, without clothing,
and have no covering in the cold.
They are wet with the rain of the mountains
and cling to the rock for want of shelter . . .
They go about naked, without clothing;
hungry, they carry the sheaves;
among the olive rows of the wicked they make oil;
they tread the wine presses, but suffer thirst.
From out of the city the dying groan,
and the soul of the wounded cries for help;
yet God pays no attention to their prayer.[5]

Now this is an important point: Job's experience has led him to realize that many people suffer in this life. At first he was just angry about his own situation, but now he is stirred up by the misery of the poor, widows, and orphans, who seem to suffer endlessly at the hands of the rich and powerful: *Yet God pays no attention to their prayer!*

Over the course of his ordeal, then, Job shifts his focus from himself to others: At the beginning of the story Job experiences intense personal suffering, including alienation and a sense of being completely cut off from humankind. But through the awareness of others' pain and the experience of compassion, he begins to feel a sense of community with other

5. Job 24:1–12.

people—if only because *everyone* suffers in some way or another. Indeed, when we encounter the suffering of another person, we are often moved by it because it makes us realize that underlying all of our differences, we are all basically the same—and at any moment something that happened to another person could also happen to me. And if we focus on this basic truth, it allows us to overcome the isolation that personal suffering brings. Have you ever helped someone or gone out of your way for another person who needed your help when you were also in distress? Paradoxically, this is one way in which your own suffering can be alleviated. And this is what Job realizes here: by focusing on the suffering of others he relieves his own anguish and personal despair.

The book of Job ends, surprisingly, with God responding to Job as the voice in the whirlwind. God seems to have no patience with Job's complaint: "Where were you when I laid the foundation of the earth?" he asks; and he describes the universe that he has created, full of strange wonders and marvels that cannot be limited to whatever is reasonable or rational. Consider, for example, the ostrich which is a very strange creature indeed:

> The wings of the ostrich wave proudly;
>   but are they the pinions and plumage of love?
> For she leaves her eggs to the earth,
>   and lets them be warmed on the ground,
> forgetting that a foot may crush them,
>   and that the wild beast may trample them.
> She deals cruelly with her young, as if they were not hers;
>   though her labor be in vain, yet she has no fear;
> because God has made her forget wisdom,
>   and given her no share in understanding.
> When she rouses herself to flee,
>   she laughs at the horse and his rider.[6]

Such wonders and marvels are truly beyond human understanding! They are not rational or reasonable in any way. And we cannot hope to understand why all the things in this life happen as they do. Hence, there is no direct answer to the problem of suffering in the book of Job, and Job's anguish is never justified or made reasonable. But by the end of the book, Job has come to realize that life is full of wonders and it can be relished

6. Job 39:13–18.

and enjoyed, even if it comes with suffering and regardless of whether that suffering can be justified or not.

At the very end of the book of Job, God chastises Job's friends and says that Job himself did well. Why is this? Isn't Job the one who challenged God? I think the problem is that Job's friends never really thought about what they were saying. I'm sure they believed they were helping Job, but in spite of Job's suffering, they thoughtlessly repeated the claim that everything is always for the best, from which it follows that Job's suffering was ultimately justified. The friends never showed Job compassion; they remained completely judgmental, and they never doubted that it was all Job's fault. On the other hand, Job tried to come to terms with what happened, and he tried to work things through. He did not avoid his pain and suffering by claiming that it was "nothing" to him, or something that he could deal with; and he did not interpret it as a part of God's plan, which would make it into something "good." We all have different ways of dealing with pain and suffering, and we have different strategies of avoidance. But Job didn't engage in this kind of self-deception. He stayed open to his suffering. And when God finally spoke, he wisely remained silent, because the justification of suffering is *not* the most important thing.

Now there are three main points that I get from this story. First, it seems to be saying that suffering is just a part of life. It is not something that has to be explained or justified, and life is not bad because people have to suffer. Job's first response is one of complete indignation and anger: I don't deserve this! Why is this happening to me? Indeed, he takes his misfortune very personally, as probably most of us would. But even though this is understandable, it is by no means the only attitude that we could take to our own suffering. For example, two patients receive exactly the same diagnosis of a terminal illness. The first patient is angry, like Job, and dwells only on the injustice of it all, shutting down his spiritual life and certain possibilities of healing. But the second patient sees the illness as an opportunity for spiritual growth. Maybe he accepts the cancer, or whatever it is, as an "act of God," or as part of his destiny, and he uses the time he has left to come to terms with his family and friends; he makes amends for any wrongs he may have committed, and he attends to his spiritual well-being.[7] Likewise, through his own suffering Job eventually experiences real compassion for others, and in this way suffering inspires his spiritual growth.

7. The example is drawn from the Dalai Lama's book, *Ethics for the New Millennium*, 138.

The second point is that Job's friends were wrong to argue that Job *deserved* to suffer. Of course, the friends did not know about the bet between God and Satan. But even so, it is a mistake to say that *anyone* should suffer, or that suffering is somehow a good thing—even if suffering is sometimes unavoidable in medical treatments, say, or in teaching us a life lesson. The worst spiritual response is trying to justify someone else's suffering; and when we say they deserve it, or it "serves them right," we become a part of the evil that we say we reject. We become judgmental like Job's friends, or the spectators who calmly allow atrocities to happen and who rationalize them as being somehow necessary and even "good." The bottom line is that in spite of any good that may come from it, suffering itself cannot be affirmed for its own sake. We should never say that someone else's suffering doesn't matter, and we should not be indifferent to suffering, even if it is the suffering of an animal or the suffering of a person who has made foolish choices in her life. Do we always know exactly what *we* are doing or what is going on? A *compassionate* response would make allowances for human ignorance and all the vicissitudes of life.

The third point is this: As we have already noted, Job's suffering leads him to become much more aware of the suffering of others. Suffering usually isolates us. It makes us feel cut off from others and pinned down to ourselves. But the author of the book of Job seems to be making the point that suffering can be a bridge that helps us to feel more sympathy for those who are struggling and in distress. For if we *can* experience compassion for others, we can ease our own anguish, and at the same time we can help others to deal with their pain. In this respect, as we will see, compassion is a basic spiritual attitude because it takes us away from our selfish point of view, and it focuses on our connection and our identity with others. Once again, we must *stay open* to suffering because it leads to spiritual growth. And so it must be accepted for what it is, without rationalization or avoidance.

Some Responses to Suffering

In this way, suffering can lead us into critical and spiritual reflection: Have I lived my life in the right way? Does my life have a purpose? Is life really worth living? We don't know much about Job before God tested him, but we assume that he was comfortable and happy with his lot. Then quite suddenly everything changed, and he was thrown into anguish and despair. Now the most urgent question for him becomes, how am I to deal with all this suffering? And how can anyone deal with such misfortune, or respond to someone else's pain? Obviously, this is a very difficult question, and over the centuries many theologians and philosophers have sought to come to grips with this issue. But taken together, I think there are at least four possible responses that can be given. Three wrong answers to start with, and then one right one.

For some people, the best response to suffering is just to "tough it out," which means becoming hard and impervious to sorrow. But this is not a good response, because in hardening ourselves—becoming fixed and stony—we also separate ourselves from all that is good and gentle inside ourselves. In a poetic passage, the philosopher Nietzsche seems to advocate this way of dealing with the world—"Become hard!" he says, for anything gentle is a form of weakness:

> The Hammer Speaks: "Why so hard? The kitchen coal once said to the diamond. "After all, are we not close kin?"
>
> Why so soft? O my brothers, thus I ask you: are you not after all my brothers?
>
> Why so soft, so pliant and yielding? Why is there so much denial, self-denial, in your hearts? So little destiny in your eyes?
>
> And if you do not want to be destinies and inexorable ones, how can you one day triumph with me?
>
> And if your hardness does not want to flash and cut and cut through, how can you one day create with me?
>
> For all creators are hard. And it must seem blessedness to you to impress your hand on millennia as on wax.
>
> Blessedness to write on the will of millennia as on bronze—harder than bronze, nobler than bronze. Only the noblest is altogether hard.
>
> This new tablet, O my brothers, I place over you: become hard![8]

As much as I appreciate Nietzsche's philosophy, I think this is a disturbing passage. For in becoming hard we become brittle and unresponsive and emotionally unavailable to others. And in such a condition I think we could justify every kind of cruelty.

Likewise, in becoming oblivious to our own suffering, we become oblivious to the suffering of other people. And we are also capable of inflicting great suffering on them because we cannot feel our own pain. For example, if we had to work in a slaughterhouse or some kind of a

8. Nietzsche, *The Twilight of the Idols*, 563.

concentration camp, our natural responses of caring would become deadened, and soon we would start to feel nothing. These are extreme cases, but in other jobs and difficult life situations, the great temptation is just to "shut down" to avoid the anguish that we experience. But this is a kind of spiritual death that closes us off to the sources of life and spiritual growth. And if we ever experience this kind of compassion burnout, we must try to remove ourselves from the situation causing it just as soon as we possibly can.

A second, related response is indifference, which some ancient philosophers have proposed as the only good strategy for dealing with pain and suffering. For if we say that nothing matters, then our pain becomes irrelevant like everything else. For the early Stoics, the art of living meant cultivating *ataraxia*, and this means becoming indifferent to the things that usually concern most people. According to the first Stoics, we are to become indifferent to pleasure and pain, poverty, illness, and even life and death. For nothing has any value apart from reason or virtue. And later, Marcus Aurelius comments: "Do not be aggrieved then if things are not always to your liking. As long as they are in accord with nature, be glad of them, and do not make difficulties."[9] I think this is a kind of "sour grapes philosophy." We are told, by the Stoics to accept whatever happens with equanimity, and to be indifferent to everything—health, personal success, love—*except* virtue, which should be its own reward. But this is like saying that life isn't that enjoyable or important anyway, so why should we get so upset if things go badly for us? Our suffering isn't relevant or important, so we should not dwell on it. Once again, this is not a spiritual response because indifference implies the rejection of life and all of its affirmative possibilities. It strongly suggests ingratitude for what we have been given and the need to avoid all that is difficult by devaluing the importance of life.

A third response to suffering—whether one's own or someone else's—is to affirm and even celebrate this suffering as a *good* thing that must ultimately be for the best. For even if we don't understand why something happened, we can still assert that it must have happened for a very good reason. In traditional religion, this kind of perspective is called theodicy, which means the justification of everything that takes place because it is all part of God's plan. This presupposes that God would never do anything that was not ultimately rational and good. The story of Job, which begins with God's bet with Satan, seems to challenge this way of thinking from the outset. Now sometimes, when something bad happens it eventually leads

9. Marcus Aurelius, *Meditations*, book XI, s. 16, 146.

to something better, which leads us to say that the suffering was justified or that everything happens for a reason: You are terribly disappointed because you did not get the job that you applied for. The one you really wanted. But a few weeks later you get an even better job than the first one, so while your initial disappointment was understandable, you should have realized that things work themselves out, and everything that happens is always for the best. But the problem with this way of thinking is that suffering *isn't* always redeemed by what happens afterwards: For example, the Holocaust of Nazi Germany was followed by other holocausts that happened later in the twentieth century. Apparently, nothing was learned from the original Shoah because genocide remains a fairly frequent occurrence. And so it seems that a lot of suffering is literally pointless; and we don't need to insist that everything has to have a meaning, or that everything is always for the best. And just as we should not avoid suffering by hardening ourselves or playing down its effects, we should not celebrate suffering either. We should simply stay open to suffering, and this brings us to compassion as the fourth response.

Compassion as a Response to Suffering

Earlier I suggested that suffering is the bottom line of human experience. What I meant is that everything changes, and so every human life is subject to disappointment, loss, and ultimately death. Of course, we may not be suffering at this precise moment if our life is going well; but at some point we are going to experience distress, or even anguish, just because that's how life is. This does not mean that life is not worth living—far from it! But we cannot ignore the reality of suffering, which shapes our lives in decisive ways, through illness, despair, and grief; while at the same time it forms a part of our everyday experience of the world: the missed opportunities and the wasted time, the wounded feelings, anguish, resentment and boredom. Suffering seems to isolate us. When we suffer a great loss, we feel completely broken and thrown back on ourselves. We are immersed in grief, and we can't just choose to think about something else. It seems that suffering is completely self-absorbing, and for as long as it continues it is hard to escape from the limits of the ego and to remain open to spiritual life. But this is why the response to suffering is so important and spiritually significant.

I believe that compassion is the most authentic response to suffering. It requires accepting suffering as a part of life; and this involves staying open to suffering instead of refusing it or denying it, or reinterpreting it as the sign of something good. In responding with compassion, I reach out to someone else. I know that she is suffering, and so I sit close to her. I give her my complete attention, and in this way I touch her pain. I will do whatever I can to help her because her suffering moves me to care for her. Such compassion is basic. Other spiritual values like love or nature can offer an exalted or more blissful kind of experience, but compassion involves an everyday connection with others that can be as simple as a smile, a gentle voice, or a respectful silence.

Compassion means "suffering with" in the sense of feeling sorrow for the suffering of another, and I believe this should be our response to suffering wherever it occurs. As we have noted, compassion is the first step toward spiritual enlightenment because it opens us up to the other person. It leads us away from our typical self-involvement and self-preoccupation by focusing on the well-being of another. And in this way, we can experience the ultimate spiritual reality—which can bring us complete inner peace—that everything is interconnected and interdependent; and there is nothing and nobody who stands completely alone. So compassion is openness to suffering: It does not reject suffering or celebrate it, but it avows it as an opening to spiritual life. This means that you should begin by having compassion for yourself, for if you are crippled by guilt or completely judgmental about your own past actions, you will remain separated from everyone and everything else. It may sound strange to put it this way, but you need to make friends with yourself. You could think about yourself as a child, when you were younger and more innocent. Can you feel compassion for your earlier self? Remember how foolish you were, and how misguided! This is not to absolve you of any responsibility; but it is surely the case that being able to feel compassion for yourself will help you to feel compassion for others. And the reverse is also true, because acts of compassion help to eliminate the sense of separation between self and others. When your suffering moves me, I care about your well-being in a very direct way. What happens to you matters to me, and I am no longer so completely self-absorbed in my own set of troubles. In feeling for you and for others, I am motivated to help you and to make your happiness a priority.

Let's think about this for a moment. We sometimes think that because of its name, compassion must involve being *passive*. It means that I am sad because you are sad and that's all there is to it. But true compassion is a spiritual *activity*. It means being open and responsive to another person;

not just viewing her as an object but thinking about her and making her needs the focus of our concern. Of course, I can't always feel what someone else is feeling; although sometimes I can put myself in their situation if I use my imagination. This is why art, film, and literature are so important: because they extend our sympathy by helping us to see things from another person's point of view. The great tragedies—*King Lear, Antigone, Oedipus Rex,* or *Hamlet*—show us the suffering and fall of great men and women whom we are bound to identify with. While novels like Dickens's *David Copperfield* or Ralph Ellison's *Invisible Man,* and autobiographies like *The Narrative of Frederick Douglass* help us to feel empathy for those who live very different kinds of lives than the one we are living now. In this way, art, literature, and film can enhance our spiritual life.[10]

So if you have suffered a great loss—a personal tragedy—then I certainly know what you are going through if I have suffered something similar. But it may also be the case that I really don't know what it is like to go through a divorce or the death of a child. In such a situation, however, I can still feel compassion for you or for any individuals, including animals, because I know what it is to suffer pain, anguish or misfortune. I can imaginatively identify with your situation, and when you suffer I can respond to you as a fellow creature, even if I don't like you or I never even met you before. The point about compassion is that it puts us in touch with the fact that at a deep level we are all basically alike. We all have the desire to be happy and to live a full life. We all want good things for ourselves and those we care about. And like everyone else, we want love, good health, and some kind of success in whatever we choose to do with our lives. In this respect, we have much more in common than we usually realize. Compassion makes us aware of this, and so it puts us in touch with our humanity.

Now we may associate compassion with pity; but it has to be said that compassion and pity are very different things. In pity we look down on someone; our pity is a kind of contempt, and self-pity involves feeling contempt and loathing for oneself. This is a terrible attitude, and it really does not help anyone! By contrast, true compassion means feeling the suffering of another and wanting to help them. And even if sometimes other responses, such as fear, make it impossible to act, the *impulse* to help is still there, and as we will see, it can be fostered. Not only through art and

10. For more on the importance of compassion, the relationship between literature and compassion, and specific readings of literary texts, see Nussbaum, *Upheavals of Thought,* esp. 297–456.

literature, but also through a variety of spiritual practices that may ultimately lead to complete self-overcoming, or what is sometimes called, in the Buddhist tradition, the "great compassion." This ideal possibility involves feeling unlimited and unconditional compassion for all of those who suffer and wherever suffering occurs. It is the point at which the selfish ego is fully overcome, although this is not experienced as a sacrifice or a loss because now we have attained a more universal point of view.

In some traditions, such as Buddhism, compassion is held to be the most important spiritual virtue because having a heart of compassion is the key to all the other virtues. And this makes sense, because we would not try to be just, courageous, or generous if we did not care about the well-being of others and their sufferings in the world. In Western culture, on the other hand, we are often told that feeling compassion is a form of weakness and "acting from emotions" when we should be acting on principle. I think this is a huge mistake. In fact, I would argue that to be compassionate is to show strength because it involves going beyond the limited horizon of our own existence to enter into the life—and the suffering—of another person. Our own suffering is oppressive. It is not something that we choose, and even though we want to escape from our suffering, we can't just decide to think about something else. But the suffering of others is something we can choose to respond to: by helping them, or saying something, or just giving them a sign to let them know they are still cherished in spite of all the suffering that oppresses them. And this can help them to recover the sense of belonging that suffering undermines. Compassion, both when it is given *and* when it is received, helps to humanize us and it makes us feel more connected to the community we belong to: the human community, the natural community, and the spiritual community of truth.

So we must stay open to suffering. We cannot harden ourselves so that we can no longer feel anything; and we should not repress our pain or claim that it is a matter of complete indifference to us. Suffering, whether our own or that of others, puts us in touch with all the complete uncertainty and impermanence of life, and this is why it is so scary and so difficult to deal with. Of course, it would be wrong to celebrate suffering and to try to justify everything bad as a really good thing. But if we could embrace change and impermanence as the underlying reality of this world, then we would be able to live with the anguish we feel because we wouldn't be afraid of it anymore. Sometimes, in the case of personal loss or physical pain, the suffering is too much to bear, at least all at once, and so we have to deal with it a little at a time. But in the end, we must welcome the suffering in. And by facing it and even leaning into it, we can learn to live with it as a part of the reality of this world.

Enhancing Compassion

Finally, then, the question is, how can we enhance our feelings of compassion? For we may not be naturally inclined to compassion, and the suffering of others may be something that we try to avoid. One spiritual practice involves the cultivation of empathy. In ancient Buddhist works, we are asked to imagine our loved ones in profound despair or torment. Try to visualize such a situation. How terrible! Now we have to imagine someone we don't know going through the same distress. This is also hard to bear. But finally, imagine your enemy or someone you don't like going through the same anguish. Put aside all negative thoughts and judgments that would draw you away from the reality of the suffering itself. At each level, you should say to yourself: "Like me, this person desires happiness but she is stricken with pain. May this person be free from suffering and the causes of suffering!"[11] In each case, the suffering is a bad thing, and by imaginatively extending empathy to everyone we can become sensitive to suffering wherever it occurs.

Tonglen is another ancient practice associated with Tibetan Buddhism that can be used to enhance our compassionate involvement with others. Basically it involves visualizing the suffering of another as a thick black smoke. Then we imagine ourselves breathing in that smoke and exhaling our own breath as a pure light that will bring that person happiness and relief from pain. At the same time we say to ourselves, "May this person be released from suffering, and may *all* people in this situation also experience relief." Although it is less widely known in the West, *tonglen* has been used for centuries as a way of experiencing our compassionate connection to other people; it undermines the boundary between self and other and in this way it keeps us *open*, even if another person's suffering is something that we typically turn away from. Once again, this is something that we can choose to cultivate within ourselves. The fact is, our moral personalities and our spiritual virtues are not fixed once and for all, because we can

---

11. See, for example, Dalai Lama, *How to Expand Love*, 140–45.

choose to enhance these things through focusing prayer and meditation, or through practices like *tonglen*.[12]

As we have seen, viewing art and reading literature are significant ways of cultivating the virtue of compassion because art and literature allow us to see things from another's point of view. In Shakespeare's *King Lear*, for example, we are shown an old man who makes foolish choices because he is old but not wise, and he doesn't understand the nature of love. As spectators in the theatre, or as the readers of the play, we come to identify with him because he is the protagonist, and we feel fear and pity for him because we have also made incredibly stupid choices in our own life. In this way, the play enhances our sense of compassion by allowing us to leave our everyday selves—if only for a short time—to imagine what it would be like to live a life that is completely different from our own. And so art and literature have a spiritual value, because they enhance our compassion and open other spiritual possibilities of life that would otherwise be unavailable to us.

Finally, you could also make an effort to stay open to your own suffering. Not by rehashing all the wrongs you have experienced in your life, and fixing on who is to blame for all this—yourself, your parents, God, or what have you. But instead, by focusing on the suffering itself as a physical and emotional sensation, detached from every rationalization. You may not be able to do this for long, but invite the pain in, contemplate it as something that is passing through you, and then let it go. Don't embrace it, but don't push it away! Sometimes when you *stop* resisting suffering or hardening yourself against it, it just goes away or it becomes something that you can learn to live with. The suffering is no longer a source of anguish, and you can accept it because now you realize that the suffering and the effort to resist it are a part of the same thing. Such a practice can be deeply transformative because it cuts away at all the fear and anguish that we associate with the suffering itself. This is also what it means to be compassionate towards yourself; for when you no longer fix yourself as an object (or a victim) determined by suffering, you are once more open to the flux of experience.

Now it must be said that compassion is not only a strategy for personal wellness and spiritual well-being. It *is* that, but at the same time it is also a way of promoting the spiritual and ethical good of humankind. Consider the past century, with its two world wars and the Holocaust; mass genocide in Rwanda, Cambodia and the Balkans; terrorism; and other conflicts. In

12. This account of *tonglen* follows Pema Chödrön's discussion in *The Places that Scare You*, 55–60.

spite of all of our technological progress, with smartphones, computers and other devices, it is by no means clear that we are making spiritual or moral progress towards ultimate reality and truth. So much of modern life is spiritually barren. The problem is that there is not enough compassion in the world, and we focus on our differences—race, religion, nationality, and ideology—or what divides us, as opposed to what we all have in common as human beings. Staying open to suffering may be the only way that we can save ourselves as a species. But this is something that must begin with individual acts of compassion and kindness, for the habit of compassion has a ripple effect: those who experience it pay it back or pay it forward to others. In this way, the spiritual life of everyone can be enhanced, and we will see in the next chapter how compassion leads to generosity.

In the first chapter of this book, I argued that spirituality may be understood on a personal level as a reorientation toward ultimate reality and truth. But at the same time it involves the whole community—the family, the nation, the world—which grows together with compassion and falls apart with acts of violence and hatred. In compassion, we care about the suffering of others, and we feel motivated to do something about their suffering because we identify with them. On the other hand, cruelty is the opposite of compassion because in cruelty we delight in the pain and suffering of another person: "It serves him right!" we say, or, "he got what he deserved." And even the suffering of innocent people can become a kind of spectacle that people enjoy. For better or for worse, however, suffering will continue to exist, and we must be open to it, instead of hardening ourselves against it. Compassion is the most basic spiritual response, and the only way we can save ourselves and the world that we belong to.

I want to finish this account of suffering and compassion with one final story from the Buddhist tradition, which is sometimes known as the Mustard Seed.[13] Kisagotami was a young woman who had a baby. She loved her baby more than life itself, but one day the child became sick and eventually he died. Kisagotami was distraught and refused to accept that her child had to die. She ran to all the healers in the village, asking for something that would bring the child back to life. Finally, she came to the Buddha: "Yes" he said "I can give you a potion that can bring your child back to life but the necessary ingredient is very hard to find." What was it? A mustard seed, but it had to be procured from a household that had never known

---

13. This story is celebrated in Buddhism. See, for example, Dalai Lama, *The Art of Happiness*, 133–34.

death. Kisagotami went from house to house begging for such a mustard seed, but everywhere she went she received the same response. For death is something that has touched everyone in one way or another, and no one could give her the mustard seed that she wanted. Eventually, Kisagotami came to realize what the Buddha had wanted her to learn—that suffering and grieving are a part of life itself, and no one is exempt from such things. She must learn to accept the grief that she shared with everyone else and begin mourning for her child. In the end, Kisagotami became a Buddhist nun, for she grasped the truth of the Buddhist teaching through the insight of her own experience. Most likely, she found that her suffering was eased when she focused her attention away from her own grief and on to the suffering that underlies all human life—for this is what brings us together as fellow creatures who share a common fate.

Suffering opens up the possibility of spiritual life. And so we must stay open to suffering, and this is the first step on the path of enlightenment. We must learn to lean into suffering with compassion. For in this way, we can experience a sense of community in the world that we belong to. Without it we would feel alienated and alone, and we would be cut off from all that really matters.

3

attention/availability
taking care of other people
openness
affirmation
FORGIVENESS

Living a Generous Life

LIFE IS GENEROUS; IT always gives itself. And showing gratitude for what we have been given is a fundamental spiritual attitude. In an absolute sense, of course, we don't "deserve" anything that we have, and we should try to lose our sense of entitlement. The world does not revolve around you, and the world does not revolve around me! Even so, we can still be grateful for the generosity and the goodness of life. There will always be setbacks, and at some point we will have to deal with sufferings both great and small. But unless we are completely traumatized, we will want to go on living, and this suggests that the underlying goodness of life is a part of our experience of it. I think that Job came to realize this much at the end of his ordeal: life is not always reasonable, or even fair, but the world is full of wonders—love, nature, friends and family, and the improbable fact of being alive—and this is something that we can be truly thankful for. Sometimes, responding to the sheer generosity of life involves thanking God—or nature itself—through prayer, service, or sacrifice of some kind. And such gratitude is *itself* a kind of generosity because it involves thanksgiving, or the *giving* of thanks. But as we will see, there are many other ways that we can participate in the generosity of the world by mirroring it in our own lives.

When people talk about *generosity* they usually mean giving away their money or giving some of their possessions to others. The philosopher Aristotle says that some people are not generous enough because they are mean-spirited and withhold their money when their friends or family really need their help. But he also says that some people are too extravagant with their gifts, and they bankrupt themselves in giving lavish presents to

35

balance

people they hardly know.[1] Hence generosity is an accomplishment—it is an ethical virtue—and it involves giving the right amount at the right time to the right people. Giving too much or too little, at the wrong time or to the wrong kind of people is not a virtue but a moral vice. I think this is the voice of common sense speaking. There is an art to giving presents, and gift-giving can be done well or badly. For example, an extravagant gift, like a new car or a diamond ring, could be overwhelming or embarrassing to the recipient if he or she is not a close friend. While meanness in giving—like giving a very modest present or leaving a small tip—suggests a reluctant generosity which can be insulting to the recipient.

Aristotle was right to say that generosity is a moral virtue. But at the same time, and at a much deeper level, generosity can also be a *spiritual* virtue because it opens us up to others and the sheer generosity of life. People can sacrifice their own well-being for the sake of someone else; and they can even give their lives so that someone else can live. Parents spend years taking care of their children and putting many of their own needs on hold. And those who look after sick or elderly relatives are also attuned in this way to the fundamental generosity of the world. We could say that they are "sacrificing" themselves for others, except that they don't even see it as a sacrifice because they are not calculating things from a selfish point of view. Of course not—it is only natural to take care of someone that we love! Sometimes we say that someone has a generous heart or a generous spirit that allows her to forgive those who have wronged her. And we may help others to flourish and thrive for their own sake, but not because of any selfish or ulterior motives that we may harbor. For the fact is, we *do* care about the well-being of other people, and so we help them; and this kind of spiritual generosity is not motivated by the desire for selfish rewards such as personal satisfaction or happiness, which are by no means guaranteed. If we do find happiness or satisfaction in helping others, this will motivate us to go on helping and giving. All of these things are forms of spiritual generosity that go beyond moral requirements, and they allow us to participate in the complete generosity of life.

The Good Samaritan

We can start to think about spiritual generosity by looking at the parable of the Good Samaritan that appears in the New Testament. This story is very

1. Aristotle's discussion of generosity is in his *Nicomachean Ethics*, book 4, 984–91.

well known, and it has helped to shape our thinking about what it means to be truly generous: A man was going from Jerusalem to Jericho when he was attacked by robbers who beat him, stripped him of everything he had, and left him for dead. A priest was coming down the same road, but when he saw the man he crossed over to the other side. Then a Levite came along and he also passed him by. Finally, a Samaritan saw the man, "and when he saw him," we are told, "he had compassion, and went to him and bound up his wounds, pouring on oil and wine." He took the man to an inn and he left money for the innkeeper, saying, "Take care of him; and whatever more you spend, I will repay you when I come back."[2]

To begin with, the story of the Good Samaritan is all about the importance of compassion, which opens us up to the suffering of another person, and inspires us to do the right thing. The priest and the Levite may have felt sorry for the man but they did not want to help or get involved. By contrast, the Samaritan showed true generosity. Even though he had never met the wounded man before, and perhaps nobody would have expected him to help, the Samaritan felt compelled to take care of him. As far as we know, the Samaritan did not take the time to think about what his moral duties were; he just stopped to help the man because here was another human being who was in distress and who needed his assistance. He was not thinking selfishly. This was just what the situation required, and so he gave the man his time and his money. He took care of him, and he made a commitment to return later to make sure that he was doing well. In fact, everything that the Samaritan did was done in the spirit of complete generosity. He did not expect a reward for what he did—either in this life or the hereafter—and he did not act out of guilt, or think about how he would feel if he *didn't* help him. He saw the wounded man, and he had to help him just because here was someone who needed to be helped.

The Good Samaritan story is an excellent example of pure generosity, when one gives oneself or does something for someone else without any expectation of return. It is important to point out that in this case, the Samaritan helped a *stranger*. If we help a friend or a family member, there are obvious reasons why we should help because our sense of well-being is bound up with theirs, and if our friends or our children suffer then we suffer too. So how could we refuse to help a relative or a friend in trouble? These obligations are unavoidable because they define who we are. But the beaten man on the road to Jericho was a stranger; and so we can say that in

2. Luke 10:30–35.

this case the helping response was a pure and unmotivated gift. The story of the Good Samaritan is put forward as an example of pure Christian love, which is also called *agape,* and it is supposed to mirror the pure love of God. Most of the time, when we love someone, we care about something in that person that appeals to us—the beauty of the one we love, or the moral character and the loyalty of our friends. The fact is, we choose our friends and our partners, but we can't love everyone as a friend, and the number of friends we can have is always very limited. We also love our children and our parents because they are *our* children and *our* parents, and we usually don't love other children in the same way that we love our own. But the most remarkable kind of generosity is to help a stranger, or to be ready to sacrifice our life for someone that we don't even know.

So while we can agree that generosity is a moral virtue, it is also a spiritual virtue on the path of enlightenment, because it involves turning away from the self or self-absorption in general and acting for the sake of others. It involves the pure gift of giving oneself away that doesn't expect any kind of return or recompense. Often when we give we remain very guarded and protective of ourselves. We know at some level that it is right to give, but we think that the more we give to others, the less we will have left for ourselves. And this scarcity mentality only perpetuates the self-other distinction that should be overcome. By contrast, living a truly generous life involves a willingness to give and receive that follows the rhythm of life and refuses to be limited by what is rational or reasonable in giving.

generosity is spiritual virtue

Enhancing Generosity

Now we saw earlier that there are some practical exercises that we can do to inspire and enhance the capacity for compassion in our own lives. The same thing applies to generosity, for all of the virtues can be trained. To begin with, you could ask yourself, what can I give away? Presumably it can't be anything that you are not attached to because then your sacrifice isn't really a sacrifice at all. So you could make a point of giving away something that you care about to benefit someone else. Can you also make generosity into a daily practice? For example, could you commit yourself to giving away one dollar every day for a whole year, or even for the rest of your life? This would force you to seek out different ways of giving, and it would enhance your sense of generosity as a more active capacity rather than just the ability to respond. You could volunteer with some local agency or charity, and in this way you could give the benefit of your skills or your expertise to those who really need it. And since gratitude is also an important aspect of the generosity of life—the ability to give *and* to receive—you could find a way to celebrate the lives of all of those who helped you to become the person you are now.

In recent years, "random acts of human kindness" and "paying it forward" have become popular ways of reflecting the generosity of the world. The former can be limited to small actions like paying the bill of the person behind you in the drive-through, or it could involve a spontaneous decision to help someone—even a stranger—who needs to be helped. Paying it forward—as opposed to paying it back—involves passing on a benefit by helping someone else, perhaps in the same way that you were helped to begin with. If someone helped you through school many years ago, then this is something that you could do for someone else. In this way, one simple act of kindness creates many others, and the world is transformed through the effects of this spontaneous generosity. This would be especially true if you decided to repay every act of kindness that you received with *three* acts of kindness to others. The ripple effect would be remarkable, and it would put us back in touch with the underlying generosity of the world. This is not about a way of repaying the original debt. It is about the possibility of spiritual renewal through connection with others and the ultimate generosity of life.

In this way, then, we can become more generous than we have been, and we can adopt practices or policies that will make us more generous to others in the future. But as we have already noted, there are other ways we can be generous and cultivate *spiritual* generosity, quite apart from giving away property or money: To start with, there is the example of taking care of other people, whether this is parents taking care of their children, or grown children taking care of their elderly parents; also, the teacher who cares for his or her students, helping them to succeed; and the friends who take care of each other. Growing more specific, however, I think there are several different kinds of spiritual generosity that we can also recognize as a potential within ourselves: For example, spiritual generosity includes giving someone your complete and undivided attention, for this requires stepping away from your own self as the center of the world and just being available to others. Such attention or availability involves giving someone else one's complete focus and one's time. This does not mean responding to someone's needs in a reactive way, although this is important too, but helping to guide a person through their difficulties and even anticipating these difficulties before they emerge. I think this is what a good teacher does, or a good parent, who gives us a strong sense of life's possibilities and how we can find fulfillment. They are always there for us, and they are usually patient when we make mistakes. The best teachers I ever had inspired me with a love of learning that will last throughout my lifetime. I am grateful to them for being available and for being concerned enough to help me make my own way through all of the difficulties of life. Likewise, a good friend is someone who is usually available to help us when we need them, and they pay attention to what we need. We always know when someone is distracted and not really paying attention to our deepest concerns. But a true friend will stand by us through all of our troubles, and will celebrate with us when life is good.

Another example of spiritual generosity would be openness, which could be openness to the future, openness to a friend or a child, or just openness to life itself. Openness means not insisting that another person has to stay exactly the same as he or she always has been, or that the future must resemble the past. It means the willingness to embrace change, and even very challenging circumstances that make it easier for another person to find herself. Sometimes it involves a willingness to question your own settled beliefs especially when the alternative would be to reject another person, dismissively, just for being *wrong*. For example, your child has just told you that he has abandoned the religion that he grew up in. You are shocked because you had no idea and this seems to go against all the values of your own upbringing. But now do you reject your child? Because you love your son or your daughter, you may want to reconsider your own fixed ideas and stay open to the possibility of change and spiritual growth. It does not mean that you are going to be happy about it, but your love for your child should help you to accept this new development. Sometimes for the sake of love or friendship, I may need to overcome my own preconceived ways of thinking, and this can be really challenging. We expect our friends and loved ones to share the same basic values that we have, but this doesn't always happen in the long run. Likewise, it can be very difficult to step back from your own position to see things from another person's point of view. But all this is openness to the other, and it is a kind of spiritual generosity that does not need to insist upon its own perspective as the only truly valid one.

Finally, another example of spiritual generosity is the power of affirmation, which involves looking at things in the best possible light that is still consistent with reality. It is a sad fact that many people are cynical and naysayers—they tend to see the worst in everything, and in this way they give us an image of ourselves as limited or flawed. By being this way, they discourage us from becoming the people we were meant to be, and they undermine the possibility that we will ever reach our full potential. In contrast, the truly generous person can give us a vision of our own higher self as a genuine possibility to pursue: And they encourage us: "This is what you were meant to do!" "I am so proud of what you have achieved, and I will support you in any way I can." Giving support and encouragement of any kind are forms of affirmation. I don't mean mindless affirmation, of course—which can be counterproductive—but whatever follows from focused attention and concern for another's well-being. Through affirmation I can show my concern, which allows another person to make the most of her life; and she will respond to this concern as a measure of her own perceived worth. Were you ever told as a child that you were stupid or that you would never amount to anything? Did you have parents who were very critical and questioned all of your ambitions as absurd or ridiculous? Or parents who had their own fixed ideas about how you should live? The point is, we all need the affirmation of others in order to flourish and thrive on our own. So affirmation is an important aspect of spiritual generosity that profoundly enhances life, and we should try to cultivate it as much as we can.

So far, then, we have looked at three different forms of spiritual generosity that could help another person to reach her full potential, or to become the person they were *meant* to be. These include *attention* or *availability*; *openness* to transformation, difficulty and change; and the power of *affirmation*. The fourth form of spiritual generosity that I want to discuss is probably more familiar. Of course I mean *forgiveness*, which by its very name suggests a profound kind of *giving*. Like generosity, forgiveness is a moral value. But once again, it is also a spiritual value especially when it goes beyond what is morally required.

The Generosity of Forgiveness

Forgiveness can be a form of self-protection that allows us to get on with our life, without feeling upset or victimized. And it is often in our own

41

self-interest to forgive. But forgiveness can also be an act of complete generosity directed towards the spiritual well-being of another person. Christianity emphasizes the absolute importance of forgiveness, both for the victim and the offender. When Jesus is asked how many times we should forgive those who continue to do us harm, he replies, not seven times but "seventy times seven times," which implies that forgiveness is *always* the best option.[3] In the New Testament, the story of the Prodigal Son epitomizes the importance of forgiveness: A father had two sons. The younger one asked his father for his share of the estate, and so his father gave it to him. Soon afterwards, the younger son left for a distant country where he squandered all of his money in "wild living." Then there was a famine, and he had to get a job feeding pigs. He was hungry, he longed to eat what he was feeding to the pigs, and so he decided to return to his father to acknowledge his sin. He imagined what he would say: "Father, I have sinned against heaven and before you; I am no longer worthy to be called your son; treat me as one of your hired servants."[4] And so he returned to his father. But when he was still some way off, his father saw him and ran to him, and threw his arms around him. The son admitted his sin, but the father, who is overjoyed, calls for his servants to bring his son his best robe and a ring, and prepare for a feast.

The older brother hears all the celebrations, and when he finds out that it is because his brother has returned, he grows angry and refuses to go in. All this time he has followed his father's wishes, but his father has never given him so much as a goat so that he could feast with his friends. And now his wayward brother is back, having squandered everything, and his father calls for the fatted calf to be killed! To which the father replies, "Son, you are always with me and all that is mine is yours. It was fitting to make merry and be glad, for this your brother was dead, and is alive; he was lost, and is found."[5]

In this story, the father forgives his son even before the son has had a chance to apologize. He does not wait for his son to come to him to beg for his forgiveness; but he runs to him, and he forgives him before he knows anything about the circumstances of his return. The forgiveness is complete and unconditional. And even though the son had concocted a plan, there is no further talk of him working off his debt as a servant. The father is

3. Matthew 18:22.

4. Luke 15:18–19.

5. Luke 15:31–32.

absolutely generous and calls for a party to celebrate the return of his child. The only person who is upset is the older brother, who feels slighted by his father's refusal to think about what the younger brother is strictly entitled to. Clearly, the older brother is diligent at keeping accounts. But this is not the right way to live, because it is not spiritually generous. It seems clear that we are meant to approve the father's generosity and kindness, but at the same time I think we may also be confused. From the perspective of justice, the older brother may be right to feel that his brother doesn't deserve anything. His brother has squandered his inheritance, as well as his life up to that point. So perhaps he does not *deserve* anything further from his family? But the father—who represents God or the generosity of life itself—forgives his son completely and unconditionally; and clearly, this is the example that we are meant to follow.

Now the question is whether this model applies to every kind of situation that involves the possibility of forgiveness. For there are different kinds of offenses, and this implies that there are also different levels of forgiveness. First, it seems obvious that when someone is rude to you but later apologizes because they were having a bad day or because they were not feeling well, you should just accept their apology and get on with your life. And if you are not prepared to forgive them, then the fault is yours for clinging unreasonably to your sense of having been wronged. In a more serious case, perhaps you were betrayed by a friend, or a spouse lied to you or abandoned you for someone else. You suffer terribly because of what this person did to you, but now he seems to be remorseful. At the same time, however, you really can't tell how remorseful he is, and you wonder if deep down he really is sorry for what he has done. In this case, it would be more difficult to forgive or forget, and I certainly don't think it is your *duty* to forgive, especially if you are still angry. In cases like this, forgiveness is more of a personal choice than a moral duty. While some people are able to move on with their lives, others find it harder to forgive such betrayals, and it is probably wrong to pressure them to forgive before they are ready to do so.

But now let's take a third kind of case, where many people would say that what happened was completely *unforgivable*: the killing of children, or our nearest and dearest; the atrocities committed by terrorists such as on 9/11 or in the Peshawar school massacre of 2014; the Holocaust of 1933 to 1945, and all the other holocausts that have happened since then—in Cambodia, Rwanda, the Balkans and elsewhere.[6] With this third sort of

---

6. Here I follow Derrida's argument in the essay "On Forgiveness" that the only true

example, we may wonder whether it would ever be just or reasonable to forgive the wrongdoer, since no amount of repentance or attempts to make amends could ever make things good again. The terrible damage has been done, and there is absolutely nothing that could ever make things right. And so it seems that we should not forgive, not just because of our own pain but also because we must never forget those who suffered or died. And to forgive is in one sense to forget.

I want to clarify this: When we think about forgiveness, we often think in terms of a debt that someone has to pay to someone else—where the offender is the debtor and the creditor is the victim. Should I forgive him? Well, that depends on how great the crime was and whether the offender feels enough guilt or has made a good enough apology. It also depends on how much goodwill I feel towards him now. The offender is indebted to the victim, who must decide how much the offender has to pay. And it is a matter of keeping good accounts—for if someone has hurt me in any way, then I am entitled to say that that person *owes* me something. Of course, we should also bear in mind the bad things that *we* have done to others, and so we should try to forgive other people for what they have done to us, because one day—inevitably—we will need forgiveness ourselves. But all of this is a kind of calculation where forgiveness is equivalent to settling a debt or keeping good credit for the future.

In ordinary circumstances, these are all very relevant considerations. But the point about forgiveness is that it is the most exceptional form of generosity when someone just cancels the debt and allows the offender to get on with his life, when he does not even demand an apology or any kind of repentance. From this perspective, forgiveness is a kind of madness because it means abandoning the account book and giving oneself away! What kind of things can be forgiven? In the final analysis, we would have to say anything and everything, and we have only to consider some recent cases to see how what is apparently unforgivable can also be forgiven. And through this kind of exceptional forgiveness the world renews itself by escaping from the endless cycle of resentment and anger that often plays itself out for several generations. Witness the recent troubles in Northern Ireland, or ethnic rivalries in Rwanda, or in the Balkans, which led to World War I and "ethnic cleansing" after the break-up of Yugoslavia. Without this kind of radical forgiveness we would remain completely stuck in the past,

---

forgiveness involves forgiving the unforgivable.

and there would be no possibility of spiritual renewal. Let us consider some of these examples.

In 1994, up to one million members of the Tutsi tribe were murdered in Rwanda by members of the majority Hutu people. A young Tutsi woman, Immaculée Ilibagiza, sought refuge in the home of a Hutu minister who was a friend of the family. For ninety-one days she hid in a secret bathroom, along with seven other women, in a space that measured only twelve square feet. The women took turns standing and stretching, and for some of the time they had to listen to the screams of people who were being killed outside. Eventually, Immaculée was able to escape to a refugee camp where she discovered that many of her close relatives had been killed, including her mother, her father, and all of her siblings except one brother. The perpetrators of this genocide included friends and neighbors and people she had grown up with. She experienced despair and rage at what had happened. But at the same time, she also knew that forgiveness was the only solution to all of the anger and grief that she felt; and as a Christian, she struggled to forgive what many people would regard as truly unforgivable.

The following passage is from the diary that Immaculée kept at that time:

> How can I forgive people who are trying to kill me, people who may have already slaughtered my family and friends? It isn't logical for me to forgive these killers. Let me pray for their victims instead, for those who've been raped and murdered and mutilated. Let me pray for the orphans and widows . . . Let me pray for justice. God, I will ask You to punish those wicked men, but I cannot forgive them—I just can't.[7]

Later, she confronted the leader of the gang that murdered her family, and she was able to forgive him, because she realized that "the love of a single heart can make a world of difference"[8]: "'What was that all about, Immaculée? That was the man who murdered your family. I brought him to you to question . . . to spit on if you wanted to. But you forgave him! How could you do that? Why did you forgive him?' I answered him with the truth: 'Forgiveness is all I have to offer.'"[9] She wanted to show compassion for someone who felt the anguish of remorse. She realized that without forgiveness she would never be whole again; and also that without forgiveness,

7. Ilibagiza, *Left to Tell*, 92–93.

8. Ibid., 210.

9. Ibid., 204.

45

her country could never have a future. Throughout her memoir, Immaculeé Ilibagiza affirms a very traditional religious standpoint, but in recent years, many people—both religious and nonreligious—have been inspired by her example to practice forgiveness in their own lives.

After the September 11th attack on the World Trade Center, a young man named Mark Stroman went on a killing rampage that lasted for several days. Calling himself "the Arab Killer," Stroman shot and killed Waqar Hasan, who was from Pakistan, and Vasudev Patel, who was from India. Both were owners of convenience stores. A third man, Rhais Bhuiyan, a Bangladeshi Muslim, survived, although his wounds left him blind in one eye. Bhuiyan said that his Muslim faith taught forgiveness, and in spite of his suffering and huge medical bills, he worked tirelessly to prevent Stroman's execution, which finally did take place in July 2011. Basically, he wanted to help Stroman by giving him a chance to redeem himself; and by showing him forgiveness and love, he eventually reached the other man's soul. As Stroman faced his execution, he was a completely changed man: "I've come from a person with hate embedded into him into a person with a lot of love and understanding for all races . . . I received a message that Rhais loved me and that is powerful." In his final moments he said, "Hate is going on in this world and it has to stop. Hate causes a lifetime of pain."[10]

In a third case, Gordon Wilson held his daughter's hand while she lay dying after a terrorist bombing in Enniskillen, Northern Ireland, in 1987. He promised himself there and then that he would forgive the bombers; and later he asked people not to take revenge for his daughter's death since that would only make matters worse. For several years and until the end of his life, Wilson worked hard to bring peace to the people of Northern Ireland, and this was his legacy to his daughter, Marie. In this case, he forgave his daughter's killers even before he knew who they were, and even before he knew if they would ever be sorry for what they had done. Many people thought he was mad, and he received some angry letters to that effect.[11] But here, as in so many other cases, including those of Rhais Bhuiyan and Immaculée Ilibagiza, the power of forgiveness is absolutely extraordinary and inspiring, and it creates a great amount of good. In Ireland, but also in South Africa, Rwanda, Cambodia, the former Yugoslavia, and other countries, the cycle of violence and retribution can only be broken if people like

---

10. See Ed Bacon's discussion of this case in his *8 Habits of Love*, 140–41.

11. For a fuller account of this extraordinary example of forgiveness, see McCreary, *Gordon Wilson: An Ordinary Hero*.

Gordon Wilson continue to press for peace and reconciliation in spite of their own personal suffering and loss. Forgiveness offers spiritual healing and renewal, and without it there is no exit from continual and repeated suffering and pain.

Forgiveness is a way of restoring our own emotional and spiritual health. For if we cannot let go of the anger that we feel because of something that happened, we will never be capable of living a truly spiritual life. And we will remain forever stuck in the past, as the *victims* of something that happened to us years ago. This is completely understandable, and not everyone has the strength to heal themselves. But the process of forgiveness has to begin at some point if we are ever going to recover our spiritual and emotional well-being. The French writer Jean Améry, like many others, refused to forgive those who mistreated and tortured him in occupied France during World War II. He suffered terribly, and he clung to his resentment as the only thing that seemed to give his life meaning until eventually he committed suicide.[12] Of course, this is a desperately tragic case, and in a situation like this I really don't think that people should be *required* to forgive because this only places an added burden upon them; and they have suffered enough. But on the other hand, if we *can* forgive, following the example of people like Gordon Wilson, Immaculée Ilibagiza, and Rhais Bhuyain, we will enlarge our sense of spiritual possibility, and recover agency in our lives. And we will be open to the complete generosity of this world.

Practicing Forgiveness and Self-Forgiveness

Forgiveness is an important form of spiritual generosity. Of course, it may not be accomplished all at once, and usually we don't just *decide* we are going to forgive someone and then do it. But we can start by setting an intention for ourselves—"I wish I could forgive him and I want to forgive him"—even if we cannot bring ourselves to forgive him quite yet. In this way, forgiveness can be a gradual process of self-overcoming and personal transformation in which we can reclaim our own life by letting go of our old selves to reach that point. By contrast, resentment and the inability to forgive tend to isolate us from others and close us off to deeper spiritual realities. And so the practical task here would be to rehearse the process

---

12. See Améry, *At the Mind's Limits*. See also, Améry's explicit discussion of forgiveness in Wiesenthal's collection, *The Sunflower*, 105–9.

of forgiveness. If you are angry with parents who mistreated you, then you could write a letter explaining your feelings, even though you will never need to send it. If you are bearing a grudge, then you could ask yourself whether anger is a justified response: People act badly out of ignorance, or because they've had an unhappy upbringing, or because they are emotionally challenged. When you understand why people do bad things, it does not justify what they do, but it helps to explain their behavior, and at that point you may start to feel compassion for them. Such compassion is one of the first steps toward the complete generosity of forgiveness. And so, if you want to forgive, but find that you can't, you can overcome your hard-heartedness by trying to understand the complete context—the upbringing, the education or lack of it, the surrounding culture, and so forth—that led someone to do what he or she did. Remember that so much of our life depends upon *moral luck*: What kind of parents did you have? What part of the world did you grow up in? What opportunities did you have when you were younger? Are you able-bodied, or do you have disabilities? None of these things are in our power, and yet so much of our life depends upon them. Sometimes, people find themselves in difficult situations where it takes an extraordinary amount of moral courage just to do the right thing. But do we *know* that we would always do the right thing if we were in that person's place? By dwelling on these kinds of issues we may start to understand that personal responsibility is a complicated and ambivalent idea, and we should cultivate compassion for those who act out of ignorance. Finally, you should always keep in mind that at some point you have probably done something bad to someone else. Something that you are ashamed of that keeps you in a state of dissatisfaction. You would like to know that you can be forgiven for what you have done so that you can have the freedom to get on with your life. But in the same way, *you* should forgive the one who offended you so that the person can have the gift of a new beginning.

By freeing us from the hurt and the anguish of the past, forgiveness helps us to recover our own life, to become the captain of our soul; it restores our inner freedom. But at the same time, we should never forget that forgiveness is one of the basic forms of spiritual generosity, and it is actually focused on the needs of another person rather than our own need. It is undeniable that you will gain a benefit from forgiving someone else, but I think that this is a happy consequence of forgiving rather than its ultimate goal. Forgiveness is not a selfish act in which I forgive *you*, and so achieve a kind of spiritual superiority and glory. Forgiveness is directed toward the well-being of another person and what he or she needs as opposed to what is easiest for oneself. It may be the hardest thing in the world, but at the same time it is spiritually empowering because it leads us away from self-preoccupation and back to the spiritual reality that anger or resentment cuts us off from. In the end, forgiveness is an extreme form of spiritual generosity that abandons the selfish perspective for the sake of another person who may be stuck in guilt and self-loathing.

Now for some people, forgiving others is actually easier than forgiving themselves for all the mistakes they have made in their own life. Once again, however, if we are not compassionate towards ourselves, we will find it much harder to be compassionate towards others, and forgiveness begins with compassion. Should we say that self-forgiveness is just a way of avoiding our responsibilities and letting ourselves off the hook? Or is self-forgiveness valuable as a way of overcoming the alienation and separation from the world that guilt and self-loathing imposes on us? An example can help us to think about the possibility of self-forgiveness in this context.

In 1971, Kelly Connor was responsible for the death of Margaret Healey, an elderly woman, in a road accident in Perth, Australia. Connor, who was seventeen years old, was driving over the speed limit and distracted as she struck Margaret Healey who was walking across a pedestrian crossing. The accident led to the breakup of Connor's family; for years she felt that she didn't deserve to live, and attempted suicide. Eventually she wrote a book about her experience, in part to help others who have been traumatized by the guilt of causing a death. Even now, she comments: "I still almost choke to say I forgive myself and sometimes I can't integrate it into my life but I've reconciled that that's how it has to be. The moment I've fixed forgiveness, it's no longer real. It has to be changing and constantly challenging. What I forgive myself for today, I don't know will apply tomorrow."[13]

It's hard to make generalizations. But in this case, Connor's guilt and self-loathing seem to be a reflection of her own moral sense. She cannot forgive herself without betraying her moral principles, for her continual guilt and self-punishment is a way of showing herself—and possibly others—that the deepest part of her is still decent and good. The problem, however, is that such self-hatred is a form of self-involvement; it prevents her from completely focusing on others, and it makes it impossible for her to be open to the absolute generosity of life. Connor has come to realize that the rest of her life was completely shaped by what happened on that

13. Cantacuzino, *The Forgiveness Project*, 141–42.

day in 1971. And while she cannot change the past, she can still revalue the meaning of the past by living a much better life in the light of this tragedy. In this case, self-forgiveness, although it remains very fragile, has allowed her to recover herself, and the endless possibilities of life itself. The self does not stand outside of the world but is a part of the world it belongs to. Forgiveness and self-forgiveness are related to each other. And the inability to forgive oneself or another can be spiritually disastrous.

Forgiveness is one of the most extraordinary things. It is a gift to the other person, which involves being willing to give her a second chance. It is a gift to the world that ends the cycle of resentment and restores the community that has been damaged. But it is also a gift to oneself in which we abandon all of our claims and our agency is restored. It is certainly an ethical achievement, but it is also a point of spiritual enlightenment. For even if we have always thought of ourselves as victims, unjustly wronged by other people, practicing forgiveness can restore the sense of being in charge of our own life, and so it enhances spiritual growth. Forgiveness is a form of spiritual generosity that reflects the endless generosity of life in all of its abundant and magical aspects, and this is something that we will talk about more in the following chapter.

I would like to end this discussion of spiritual generosity by looking at the Buddhist story of the Hungry Tigress, which is one of the legends associated with the previous incarnations of the Buddha. The story of the Hungry Tigress is an ancient legend concerning the true nobility of self-sacrifice: The three sons of King Maharatha—Mahapranada, Mahadeva, and Mahasattva—were strolling together in a beautiful park through a large thicket of bamboo. Two of the brothers were afraid because they thought there might be some dangerous animals there, but Mahasattva's heart was filled with happiness. He muses to himself: "My heart is filled with bursting joy for soon I'll win the highest good."[14] In the thicket the princes see a tigress surrounded by five young cubs. She was hungry and exhausted, and the brothers were full of compassion for her. They knew that she would die soon and they really wanted to help her, but self-sacrifice was difficult: "Yes" Mahasattva said:

> It is difficult for people like us, who are so fond of our lives and bodies, and who have so little intelligence. It is not at all difficult,

14. The story of "The Bodhisattva and the Hungry Tigress" is in Conze, *Buddhist Scriptures*, 25.

however, for others, who are true men, intent on benefitting their fellow-creatures, and who long to sacrifice themselves.[15]

Even so, as they approach the tigress, Mahasattva decides that he will sacrifice his life for her. He asks his brothers to leave him alone for a while and then he makes the following vow to sacrifice himself and to alleviate the pain of others:

> For the weal of the world I wish to win enlightenment, incomparably wonderful. From deep compassion I now give away my body, so hard to quit, unshaken in my mind. That enlightenment I shall now gain, in which nothing hurts and nothing harms, and which the Jina's sons have praised. Thus shall I cross to the Beyond of the fearful ocean of becoming which fills the triple world.[16]

Mahasattva throws himself in front of the tigress but she is too weak to move. And so he cuts his own throat with a piece of bamboo. The tigress is stirred by the prince's body all covered in blood, and in no time at all she eats up all the flesh and blood, leaving only the bones.

This story—we can call it a parable—is strange and excessive, but I think this is quite deliberate. Out of profound love for the whole of creation, the young Prince Mahasattva sacrificed himself for the tigress. He didn't really ask himself whether such a sacrifice was reasonable or required of him—indeed his brothers commented that there was nothing to be done. But in giving his life for the tigress, he gave himself completely, and without the expectation of return. We might say that in this case, Mahasattva's generosity is truly excessive because it goes beyond every moral expectation or requirement. But the whole point about generosity is that it is *always* exceptional. True generosity is astonishing because it always exceeds whatever is reasonable or required, meaning that no one can be *obliged* to be generous. This is why generous actions are surprising because they are always unexpected and derive from the complete spontaneity of life. As we sometimes say, "you didn't have to do that." Generosity is the point at which an individual gives himself to another and in this way, for a while at least, he or she can overcome the limitations of selfhood that are usually so constraining. Would you sacrifice your life for a hungry tiger? Common sense might say that this is absurd, but perhaps the whole point of the parable is to show that by giving or sacrificing himself Mahasattva

15. Ibid.
16. Ibid., 26.

was able to overcome his selfish limitations, and in this way he came to reflect the principle of generosity, which is the principle of life itself. In the end, it can no longer be considered a sacrifice because he is now at one with everything that is. Having achieved the supreme level of generosity, he no longer exists as a separate being. He has overcome his selfish motivation and he has achieved enlightenment.

Living a generous life involves more than just giving someone money—although it may certainly include this. It also involves caring for others, which includes attention and availability, the power of affirmation, and openness, among other things—as well as forgiveness, which may well be its most extraordinary manifestation. This is the second step on the path of enlightenment that we must make our own. For when we live generous lives, we are most completely attuned to the fundamental generosity of life. In fact, we *become* the generosity of the world; and this is a profoundly spiritual achievement.

4

Cultivating Mindfulness and Wonder

IF WE THINK ABOUT spirituality and what it means to live a spiritual life, we should also think about what a life completely *lacking* in spirituality might be like. Presumably, the opposite of a spiritual life is one that is totally self-absorbed and concerned with ordinary values like material success, popularity, and power. A "nonspiritual" person wouldn't care about other people or experience a positive sense of belonging to anything that was greater than her own existence. She would not be able to respect spiritual values like art, religion, music, or the truth, and she would never be astonished or seized by a sense of wonder at the beauty of nature or the starry sky at night. She would never forgive unless it was in her own best interest to forgive, and she would not feel compassion or even know how to love another person.

Is such a life possible, or would it even be a human life as we know it? This is debatable. The problem is that in modern life we seem to be getting closer to this point. A lot of things have improved for us in the past two hundred years. In the West, at least, more and more people have a reasonable standard of living, and consumerism is rampant with the availability of many products and devices that should save time and allow us to live our lives more fully. Education and healthcare have improved significantly; people can earn enough to support themselves and their families. And yet, somehow, things have gone wrong. We often find ourselves distracted and unfocused, and the popularity of the Internet, Facebook, and smartphones hasn't helped us with matters of ultimate concern. We are plugged into all kinds of devices, but we are separated and alienated from the real world of nature. We are no longer very mindful of what we are doing, and we have lost a sense of wonder. Especially in this information age, we only consider facts and opinions. The world has become disenchanted as science pushes out all nonscientific explanations as fanciful or vague. And for the most part, we no longer even recognize the possibility of wisdom unless this is something that can be reduced to information, or quantified like the results of a consumer survey.

All of this involves the reduction of spiritual life to just another "life choice" that is neither more nor less valid than any other way of life—or at least this is what we tell ourselves. But at a deeper level, we know that something isn't right. In spite of all of our wealth and our technological achievements, we are not happy with what we have. Addiction of one kind or another has become a massive social theme, and we often use drugs, alcohol, food, work, and online activity to stifle the anguish of spiritual oblivion. In spite of our irony and scoffing at spiritual themes, we still look forward to a more meaningful life. But since this is *not* associated with plea-sure, money, or even personal success, we really don't know how to make sense of this possibility. And for as long as we are not focused on things that really matter, we are bound to feel like the prisoners in Plato's cave—for we are squandering our lives, and cut off from that which is most important and also more real than anything else.

Art, Love, and Being Present

As we have already noted, however, a spiritual life does not need to be fo-cused on heaven or any kind of afterlife. In fact, one of the goals of a truly spiritual life is just to be more deeply involved in *this* life: To appreciate and be thankful for what we have been given, and to cultivate a sense of wonder that puts us in touch with matters of ultimate concern. Usually, we have to work for spiritual goods; but sometimes we are simply *given* this kind of experience. When we fall in love, for example, we can begin to feel a sense of wonder at everything that we encounter. For love opens us up to all the mysteries of life, and it leaves us with a powerful sense of the world as an astonishing and miraculous place. In love we are overwhelmed by the mystery of another person, and the luminosity of another life that can never be mine.

I will say more about love later. But the same thing is also true of art. Artists and poets look at this world, which sometimes seems flat and stale because of our habitual ways of thinking and responding. And they cut through all of these routine layers to create a new perspective on things, which is both astonishing and real. It is not that art—or literature—creates a *new* world that we can escape to. But the power of art helps to illuminate the world that we belong to, even if all of our habitual responses seem to obscure it from view. Think, for example, of the paintings of Cézanne, Monet, and Van Gogh, which make us aware of the pure radiance of nature and light; Brueghel's *Crucifixion* or Michelangelo's marvelous depiction of God giving life to Adam, which show the meaning of suffering and creation; or more recent artists like Francis Bacon, Anselm Kiefer, and others, who challenge spiritual ideas in a spiritually provocative way. Art celebrates life, and it makes us more aware of the beauty of the world around us. And in ways that I don't think we completely understand, art can also uncover the deepest truth about the world by triggering spiritual possibilities that are otherwise hidden from view. Today philosophy remains a fringe activity; religion is still popular, but it has fixed ideas about this world and the next, and it is not always capable of inspiring subjective thought. But art remains a very powerful force in the sense that art continues to stir the soul in significant ways—with paintings, music, films, operas, novels, architecture and poetry. And in this respect, the artist is a kind of spiritual seer, because he or she is able to escape the ordinary perspective of everyday life. In fact, it would probably be true to say that artists have become the spiritual leaders of our time. We look to writers, painters, and musicians for inspiration and spiritual guidance. Artists reflect on the deeper meaning of life, and in their work they strive to convey all the turmoil of their search as well as the insights they have achieved.

The great work of art inspires us with spiritual possibilities. It recalls us to the deepest level of our being, and it helps us to reflect on profound spiritual themes, including love, compassion, suffering, and the value of life. The romantic poet Percy Shelley says that poetry or art "lifts the veil from the hidden beauty of the world, and makes familiar objects be as if they were not familiar," while other writers identify art with the transfiguration of the world.[1] I would say that art puts us in touch with the spiritual order of the world, and it helps us to recognize the beauty of things around us. In fact, art, as well as love, helps us to focus on the absolute value of the present moment, which is something that often escapes us. In love, we can experience moments of pure presence and freedom from everything that

---

1. Shelley, "A Defence of Poetry," 563. See also, Danto, *The Transfiguration of the Commonplace.*

draws us away from life. And in the true experience of art, we put aside our everyday projects and goals as we immerse ourselves in whatever drama, symphony, painting, or film commands our complete attention. So with art and love it is possible to live more completely in the present moment. By contrast, for much of the time we live in regret about the past. We cannot have done with things, and so we are oblivious to what is actually happening *now*, and the present is poisoned by the past. Sometimes we just muddle through our lives because we are looking forward to some future point—after school, after work, or after this life is over. But this way of thinking also undermines the value of the present by making it into a means to an end that may never actually come.

The philosopher Nietzsche realized this much in his famous parable or thought experiment that is known as the eternal recurrence. The idea of eternal recurrence is a provocation, and it is meant to bring us back to the present moment as something that must be valued for its own sake:

> The greatest weight.—What, if some day or night a demon were to steal after you into your loneliest loneliness and say to you: "This life as you now live it and have lived it, you will have to live once more and innumerable times more; and there will be nothing new in it, but every pain and every joy and every thought and sigh and everything unutterably small or great in your life will have to return to you, all in the same succession and sequence—even this spider and this moonlight between the trees, and even this moment and I myself. The eternal hourglass of existence is turned upside down again and again, and you with it, speck of dust!"
>
> Would you not throw yourself down and gnash your teeth and curse the demon who spoke thus? . . . Or how well disposed would you have to become to yourself and to life to crave nothing more fervently than this ultimate eternal confirmation and seal?[2]

Nietzsche was a spiritual philosopher. Even though he denied the traditional idea of God and famously proclaimed "the death of God," he affirmed the sacred character of this life here and now; and he believed that traditional religion had diminished this world in favor of the illusory possibilities of the life to come. Here in the parable of the eternal recurrence, Nietzsche imagines a life that you cannot escape from, for there is no afterlife and no final oblivion. The only thing that exists is this life, with every present moment repeated endlessly for the rest of eternity. But how are we to deal

2. Nietzsche, *The Gay Science*, 341.

with all of this? In this thought experiment, two possibilities are suggested. First, we may respond to the endless repetition of every action and every minute detail as if it were the most extreme form of nihilism, which leads to absolute despair. For what is the point if we never get anywhere and we are always brought back to this moment? But on the other hand, if we *could* change ourselves and learn to cherish the present moment for its own sake (and not just as something to be endured), we would feel the joy of being completely at *one* with existence itself. Every moment is unique, and we must be open and receptive to it. A truly spiritual person affirms existence in the present; and like the artist or the lover—who lives in mindfulness and wonder—he or she is capable of responding to the sacred dimension of life which is always here and now.

Life as Mystery and Miracle

I want to develop some of these points, and I believe we can look more closely at the ideas of mindfulness and wonder by thinking about the story of Mojud, which is a legendary Sufi tale.[3] Mojud is described as "the man with the inexplicable life," and his story focuses on the wonder of life itself, or the "magical" dimension of the world: Once upon a time there was a man called Mojud who was the inspector of weights and measures in a small town, and it seemed more than likely that he would spend the rest of his life in that position. One day, while he was walking through the Sufi gardens, the mysterious Sufi, Khidr, appeared to him and told him to leave his job and meet him at the riverside in three days' time. When Mojud gave up his position, the people thought he had gone mad, but they soon forgot all about him and someone else was appointed in his place. On the day that had been set, Mojud met Khidr, who told him to tear his clothes and jump into the river. He added, "Maybe someone will save you." Mojud did so, wondering if he really was mad. He drifted a long way but eventually a fisherman pulled him into his boat, and took him to task for risking his life. Mojud could not explain what he was doing, but he went to live with the fisherman for a few months. He taught the fisherman how to read and write and helped him with his work, and in return the fisherman looked after him. Then Khidr appeared to Mojud again and told him to leave the fisherman, assuring him that he would be well provided for. That same day

3. Mojud's story is "The Man with the Inexplicable Life" in Shah's collection, *Tales of the Dervishes*, 155–57.

Mojud met a farmer, whom he stayed with for two years; and during this time he learned a great deal about agriculture. Eventually, Khidr appeared again and told him to walk to Mosul to become a skin merchant. Mojud obeyed. He became successful, and he was just about to buy a house for himself when Khidr appeared once more, telling him to leave his money and walk out of the city as far as Samarcand. Mojud did as he was told and eventually he began to show signs of illumination. He healed the sick and his knowledge of the mysteries grew more and more profound. Clerics wanted to know who his teacher had been, but he could not tell them. They wanted him to write the story of his life. And so he told them how everything had happened, beginning with his jumping into the river and ending with his journey to Samarcand. But the people were not satisfied because the story did not explain any of his wonderful gifts or his example. And so, we are told, "the biographers constructed for Mojud a wonderful and exciting history; because all saints must have their story, and the story must be in accordance with the appetite of the listener, not with the realities of the life."[4]

In this fantastic tale, Mojud shows complete trust in the goodness of life. He is bewildered by what he is asked to do, and all the changes he has to make, but at the same time he does not try to control his destiny. He has reached a successful position as the inspector of weights and measures, but he remains open to the possibility of change, and he does not cling to the comfortable life that he is used to. Through his willingness to follow the commands of Khidr, and the dictates of fate, he becomes spiritually accomplished and highly respected as a figure of wisdom. In effect, the story is saying that life is full of wonders and we should be open to the mystery that it offers to each one of us. We should not just calculate the possibilities that life seems to offer from our own narrow vantage point, but we should remain open to all the hidden laws and fateful coincidences that happen to come our way. Of course, the whole thing is a parable, or a fairy tale that even the author refuses to take seriously—especially since Mojud is not a particularly heroic figure of the sort who imposes his will on the world. But he is open to the miraculous and the magical; and he respects all the subtle workings and complex interactions of life, whatever its final goal is and whatever part he has to play in it.

The story affirms that the world is full of wonders and miracles both great and small. But in our everyday distraction, we fail to notice them, or

4. Ibid., 157.

we notice them only when they are literally unavoidable. Take the example of nature: for much of the time we treat the natural world as if it were merely an object that only exists for our benefit. We think of nature as something that we can dominate and control: Nature is the garden that we tend and cultivate, the source of fruits and vegetables, and even animals that people consume as food products. In this sense, nature is not threatening, and usually we only notice it when it becomes difficult or unmanageable—in the case of a tornado, an infirmity or a disease, or a wild animal that crosses our path. But at the same time, whenever we feel upset and alienated from the world we live in, we may want to spend some time in natural surroundings, in a forest or a wilderness, by a river or an ocean or any other place of great natural beauty. For this helps us to feel restored to ourselves and at home again in the world, which can be encountered as a magical place. Likewise, we can experience the tremendous power as well as the astonishing beauty of nature. Looking out at a storm at sea, for example, or watching the migration of birds, or other animals that delight and inspire us. When we look at the starry sky at night, we become aware of the immensity of the cosmos and our own minuteness by comparison. If we go into the desert, where there is no noise or light pollution, such an experience can be especially transformative. But even though these sorts of experiences seem to undermine our ordinary ways of looking at the world, they are absolutely affirmative experiences, for we come away from them with an enhanced life and a sense of belonging to something that is much greater than we are. Unfortunately, such things are becoming increasingly rare, given our own distracted lives. But the fact that they are still possible—through nature, art and love—is a sign that we are *spiritual* beings and we are oriented towards spiritual fulfillment.

So far, I have spoken about the sense of wonder, which is an important part of spiritual life: Mountains, canyons and oceans, animals, trees and beautiful flowers—here the experience of nature is paramount. There are also special experiences that pull us out of our ordinary routine and give us a strong sense of the sacred character of life—the birth of a child, or a near-death experience, the feeling of love, and especially love at first sight. Such exceptional experiences seem to open up the hidden nature of the world for us. In fact, it can be said that the world is full of miracles. I don't just mean the grandiose miracles that are described in the Bible—the parting of the Red Sea or the burning bush—but everyday miracles of kindness and forgiveness, and even ordinary things—like children playing, a song overheard, a dog barking, or a mural on a street wall—which seem to connect us to the pure generosity of life. I believe a truly spiritual person is someone who is attuned to such miracles, and she delights in them as much as anything else. For her, the world is never an ordinary place, but the extraordinary setting for marvels and wonders that testify to the sacred character of *this* life, as it can be experienced here and now.

Wassily Kandinsky, the famous twentieth-century artist and the pioneer of modern abstract painting, tells us an interesting story in an autobiographical essay that he wrote.[5] Kandinsky was a devout Christian, and by all accounts he was a profoundly spiritual person. He was also a brilliant man, accomplished in several fields. At the age of thirty he was offered a position as a professor of law, and he agonized over whether he should take the position or not. Eventually, he decided to devote his life to painting, but for a long time he wondered whether he had made the right decision. Kandinsky loved Russia, but after he became a full-time painter he moved to Munich to study art. In his essay, he describes how as a child in Russia he played for hours and hours with his favorite toy horse, which had very distinctive yellow markings. Years later, after he had moved to Munich, he was astonished to see a real horse that exactly resembled his childhood toy with the same unusual marks. For a long time afterwards, he would encounter this horse on the street, and he came to think of it as an "immortal" because it never seemed to age. But was the appearance of this horse just a "coincidence," as many people would say? For Kandinsky it was a sign that he was on the right path; and the horse seemed to give him back his childhood by connecting Munich to his early life in Russia.

Now whatever we may say about this story, I think it shows how Kandinsky himself was completely attuned to the magical dimension of life, which resists cynicism and irony and the completely "rational" explanation of everything that happens. In his artistic manifesto, *Concerning the Spiritual in Art*, Kandinsky argues that the *refusal* of miracle and mystery is one of the features of modern existence that confirms the oblivion of spiritual life, or the disenchantment of the world. In fact, "It is the condition that nothing mysterious can ever happen in our everyday life that has destroyed the joy of abstract thought. Practical considerations have ousted all else."[6] Kandinsky rejected the "nightmare" of materialism which "has turned the

5. Kandinsky, "Reminiscences."
6. Kandinsky, *Concerning the Spiritual in Art*, 99.

life of the universe into an evil useless game."[7] He always experienced the full mystery of life, and this, in part, is why he became such an important spiritual artist.

A second example of what I am talking about comes from the life story of the American Indian holy man, Black Elk. Black Elk was born a Lakota Sioux in 1863, and he came of age during a turbulent period of American history, when the Sioux lost their traditional way of life and were forced to live on reservations. In the book *Black Elk Speaks*, he describes many events that he witnessed or participated in, including the Battle of the Little Bighorn and the death of General Custer, the killing of Crazy Horse, and the massacre at Wounded Knee. But more personally significant than any of these things, when he was a young boy of about nine years old, he had an incredible dream, or a vision, which stayed with him all his life; and he came to think of this dream as the most important thing that ever happened to him. The dream involved a very detailed vision of the Six Grandfathers, who seemed to represent the four directions, heaven, and earth; different-colored horses dancing and speaking to the tribe; the people in procession; and the four virgins, who were "more beautiful than women of the earth can be."[8] Finally, there was the "sacred hoop" and the "flowering tree," which seemed to represent the unity of his people and the unity of all beings in the oneness of life. The dream is recounted over the course of several pages, but a short excerpt will help to bring out the *magical* quality of Black Elk's experience:

> Then a Voice said: "Behold this day, for it is yours to make. Now you shall stand upon the center of the earth to see, for there they are taking you."
> I was still on my bay horse, and once more I felt the riders of the west, the north, the east, the south, behind me in formation as before, and we were going east. I looked ahead and saw the mountains there with rocks and forests on them, and from the mountains flashed all colors upward to the heavens. Then I was standing on the highest mountain of them all, and round about beneath me was the whole hoop of the world. And while I stood there I saw more than I can tell and I understood more than I saw; for I was seeing in a sacred manner the shapes of all things in the spirit, and the shape of all shapes as they must live together like one being. And I saw that the sacred hoop of my people was one of

7. Ibid., 6–7.
8. Black Elk, *Black Elk Speaks*, 41.

many hoops that made one circle, wide as daylight and as starlight, and in the center grew one mighty flowering tree to shelter all the children of one mother and one father. And I saw that it was holy.[9]

In modern life we tend to dismiss visions and dreams as insignificant or unreal, and certainly *less* real than our ordinary waking reality. But for Black Elk, the dream was a powerful spiritual message that could not be ignored. Black Elk did many things in his life, but he came to believe, through his "great vision," that his task was to restore the sacred hoop of the people, and in this way to bring about the renewal of American Indian culture.

Later, the medicine man Black Road tells Black Elk that the whole tribe must reenact the dream in all of its details, to make it into an objective reality that everyone would be able to experience. "Then he said to me: 'Nephew, I know now what the trouble is! You must do what the bay horse in your vision wanted you to do. You must do your duty and perform this vision for your people on earth.'"[10] Again, the description of the ceremony is powerful and compelling; and once the Horse Dance is completed everyone feels much happier and more united as a community, for what had been a private experience is something that now belongs to all of them. For Black Elk, the dream or the vision that he had as a young boy was a profound spiritual experience that ordered his whole life and gave his life an overarching sense of spiritual purpose. But such visions and dreams are becoming rare; and even when they do happen, how often do we listen to them or take them seriously as anything more than "just a dream"?

The point is, spiritual life requires a sense of wonder that allows us to remain open to spiritual experiences and to be transformed by them. For without a sense of the miraculous we would find the world a very ordinary place in which ordinary ideas and established ways of thinking must always prevail. Without a spiritual imagination we would only love someone if it was reasonable to do so, and other spiritual themes such as generosity, compassion, and forgiveness would be based entirely on self-interest. But a spiritual life is *not* a selfish life. A spiritual life involves a sense of attunement to spiritual values and openness to the cosmos itself—as in the case of Mojud, who is ready to change his life and trusts himself to fate whenever this seems to be required of him. So we must have a sense of wonder, but we must also have complete mindfulness about whatever we are doing. Mindfulness means being completely present and concentrated

9. Ibid., 43.
10. Ibid., 161.

in the present moment, and doing everything in a focused and thoughtful way. We cannot live in a state of distraction! For then we simply lose ourselves, and we become impersonal beings, driven by the demands of consumerism and other ordinary pressures—to be "successful," to own all the right products, or to be popular with many friends on Facebook. All of which is a kind of spiritual death.

The Practice of Mindfulness

So how are we to achieve mindfulness? And how do we avoid distraction and addiction to find a sense of purpose in our lives? Every spiritual (and religious) tradition has a set of practices or techniques that allow individuals to cultivate their spiritual powers. For example, in Buddhism and other Asian traditions, meditation is used as a way of promoting mindfulness, which returns us to the spiritual path we have chosen to live by. In Christianity, Islam, and Judaism, prayer is used to step away from our ordinary life and to focus our attention on God or on something that is much greater than we are. In the Indian tradition of yoga, the aim is to achieve a "spiritual body" and harmony between the various aspects of our being, so that we are not at war with ourselves or divided between physical and spiritual goals. In Zen Buddhism, teachers use koans, or verbal puzzles, to force novice monks and students to think beyond established paths of thinking and to cut through all of the fixed ideas they have about the world: The novice is told to think about *the sound of one hand clapping*; or the question is raised: "If you meet someone along the road who has realized the truth, you may not walk past the person in silence, nor speaking. So how should you meet this person?"[11]—In each case, the goal is *mindfulness*, which is the necessary accompaniment to spiritual experience itself. For even if you have a tremendous spiritual experience, its power to transform you will diminish and ultimately die unless you are focused on your spiritual life and thoughtful about how you are living in the present. Obviously, some people are more comfortable with certain techniques as opposed to others. But the important point is that following some kind of spiritual practice in an ongoing way is crucial for developing a spiritual life; for we cannot rely on spiritual enthusiasm, which rises and falls from one day to the next.

11. For a good selection of Zen koans, see Reps and Senzaki, compilers, *Zen Flesh, Zen Bones*.

We can look more closely at the practice of meditation. Meditation has always been important in Asian wisdom traditions, although it is not central in Judeo-Christian thought. One of the chief goals of meditation—at least as practiced by Buddhist and Hindu practitioners over hundreds of years—is to become more completely aware of what is going on inside of our minds. Meditation—whether seated or walking—may begin by focusing on breathing, the rhythmic inhalation and exhalation of breath which promotes a kind of calm openness to everything that is. We must focus on the in-breath, hold it in for several seconds, and then exhale. Think about nothing else but the steady process of breathing: inhale, exhale, inhale, exhale, and so on for several minutes. As this goes on we may eventually achieve a quiet mind.

Next, we can try to witness what is actually going on inside of our heads: vague fragmentary thoughts, a confusion of different feelings, hope, sadness, anxiety, contentment, fear. We should let these thoughts and feelings well up; we should observe them, and then let them pass away again. We may become physically uncomfortable or distracted, but we should keep returning to the meditation. It soon becomes clear that none of our responses are fixed or immutable. The fact is we can choose to cultivate positive emotions such as gratitude and compassion while downplaying negative emotions including anger, hatred, or jealousy as responses that we don't want to affirm as our own. Sometimes in life we are just thoughtless and reactive. If someone says something hurtful, I may instinctively respond with anger. But how appropriate is my angry response? Am I just frustrated at this point in the day, or am I overreacting because I don't understand where the other person is coming from? And is it good for anyone if I foster my anger? Perhaps I should just observe it and allow it to pass without embracing it as "mine." And if we are willing to meditate and be more attentive to the whole range of our experience, then soon we may come to realize just how many of our responses are the products of false beliefs or unreflective patterns of thinking. Eventually, this leads to an experience of serenity, which involves pure mindfulness and a sense of detachment from the world—which is not the same thing as indifference or the avoidance of life. The spirit of meditation is not a form of escapism but a way of engaging more deeply with life itself.

Prayer is another kind of mindfulness training. In prayer, we express our gratitude and devotion; we focus our attention on what really matters to us—the safety of loved ones or those we don't even know. We ask that we may become better people and live up to a certain positive image that we have of ourselves. In the famous "Serenity Prayer," for instance, we focus on becoming aware of our own limitations, trusting in life, and doing whatever we can to improve our spiritual situation:

> God, grant me the serenity to accept the things I cannot change,
> the courage to change the things I can,
> and the wisdom to know the difference.[12]

The prayer makes us mindful of who we are, and it promotes a sense of humility, courage, and trust. In prayer we give ourselves a spiritual direction, and this allows us to step aside from all the anxiety, grief, and regret that characterize our everyday mental process. In prayer, as in the Serenity Prayer above, we also make intentions about how we are going to live our life; for in talking to God, or whatever we admit to being greater than ourselves, we are forced to be authentic and honest. Prayer helps us to accept our misfortune, to become more available and loving to others, and to come to terms with all the hardships that we face. And like meditation, prayer is a way of becoming more mindful of our own inner life; it allows us to make sense of what is happening and it helps us to realize what we have to do about it.

All of this puts our life into a much broader perspective. Mindfulness is an individual practice, but it is also a way of life. And especially today, when we are much more likely to think of ourselves as members of a global community that transcends more narrow affiliations such as nationality, religion, or class. To live mindfully is to consciously practice acts of kindness and compassion, which testifies to our connection to all beings and our identification with them. It is to protect the earth by living frugally, not wastefully, and not polluting the world with rubbish. It is also to think of our own life as a model or an example that others could follow, promoting peace and harmony, forgiveness, and love.

So just as there are different ways of getting physical exercise, such as walking, running, or swimming, there are also different forms of spiritual exercise, including meditation, prayer, *tonglen*, or just walking the dog in a mindful way. No one way is inherently better than another. It just depends on whatever works for you. The important thing is to have some

---

12. The Serenity Prayer is attributed to the theologian Reinhold Niebuhr. It has become important in Alcoholics Anonymous and other twelve-step movements. See Pietsch, *The Serenity Prayer Book*.

form of spiritual practice as a constant in your life. Meditation and prayer are two important forms of spiritual centering. They help us to enhance our spiritual response so that we can live more authentically. It seems obvious that spiritual life involves spiritual experiences; but at the same time, unless we practice mindfulness, through meditation, prayer or some other discipline, we may not be able to incorporate these experiences into our life, and we won't be empowered or transformed by them over the course of our lifetime. One very obvious example of what I'm talking about here is love. Love is an exceptional experience. It can open us up completely to the goodness of life, and it can give us a sense of being at one with everything that is. It can be a force of great spiritual inspiration or—in some unhappy cases—it can lead to obsession and self-abandonment. It is certainly based on wonder, but as Plato makes clear it can either be a stepping stone to a fuller spiritual life or a kind of narcissism that is spiritually disastrous.

Love as a Spiritual Theme

Let us think some more about the spiritual aspects of love. Love is an everyday miracle and a thing of wonder. And every kind of love is astonishing and miraculous when experienced from within. In love we regard the other person with a sense of awe. The loved one is not just another object that I can control and relate to—like a table or a chair—but an infinite being that I will never completely know. The beloved continually delights and surprises me. I am usually the center of my own life, and the subject of my own experience, but in love—whether this is romantic love, parental love or even friendship—I experience the priority of another person. In this respect, love of any kind can be an astonishing experience, for it forces me to revalue my life, and to change my priorities about what I think is most important to me. Love is a spiritual experience that can be profoundly transformative of who I am. It requires abandoning the ordinary perspective on life with all its false values of material success, popularity, and power, and it forges a connection to something that has much greater value and importance. Often love involves sacrifice and the realization that my own existence is secondary since I am willing to die for the ones that I love.

In the *Symposium*, one of Plato's most important dialogues, Socrates describes the "ladder of love," which is a path of spiritual understanding and development that begins with the experience of physical desire and love.[13]

13. Plato, *Symposium* 210a–212b.

This is what he has learned from the priestess Diotima: Most of the time we are self-absorbed and cheerfully self-contained. We look at the world as an object to be known and used, and we are basically alone with ourselves. But then we encounter a beautiful individual, and we are pulled away from ourselves and our habitual self-preoccupation as we become fascinated or even filled with yearning for the other person. According to Socrates, love is the first intimation of eternity, for it gives us the sense that the everyday world is not enough for us and there is another realm—a spiritual realm—that somehow transcends the ordinary world we live in. This is what we realize when we love someone else, and especially when we fall in love: a sudden glimpse or a revelation of eternity.

Socrates warns us, however, that love of individual beauty is not an end in itself. Of course, people can become preoccupied or even obsessed with a single individual; but, he argues, the natural goal of love is to open our spiritual horizons and put us in touch with a higher and more significant reality than the one that usually concerns us. And so we must be mindful of what is happening, or we will remain at the most basic level without making any spiritual progress. In the *Symposium*, Socrates claims that the love of individual beauty must eventually lead to the love of *all* physical beauty. For once we are opened up to spiritual life, we are bound to appreciate the beauty that is everywhere in the world—in nature, in art, as well as everyday life. The artist, for example, is someone who uses her eyes, and she is capable of seeing beauty wherever it occurs. At this point, it is not that we can no longer love specific individuals, but the love of individual beings allows us to enter a broader realm of concern. Perhaps we knew this already, for being in a loving relationship helps you to love others; and in love, as the poet Shelley puts it, "to divide is not to take away."[14]

After the love of individual beauty and the love of all physical beauty comes the love of moral beauty. Not everyone (or everything) is physically attractive, but we come to realize that some people have an inner beauty that belies or transcends their outward appearance. They have beautiful souls, and according to Socrates, we are able to recognize this moral beauty only because we already appreciate the physical beauty of the world. Regardless of any blemish or affliction, we enjoy being with such people because we are attracted by the power of goodness. In this way, beauty becomes a stepping-stone to morality. And from the love of beautiful souls we are led to the love of beautiful principles—including morality, truth, and even

14. Shelley, "Epipsychidion," 415.

mathematical and scientific laws—that structure the universe we belong to. These are higher things, and if we have followed the transformations of love then we are bound to recognize the hold that these things have over us. Presumably this is why some people can be in love with the truth or are capable of speaking truth to power in spite of the danger it puts them in— Socrates, Gandhi or Martin Luther King Jr. are obvious cases in point. And this is why we are dedicated to moral principles—do not lie, do not steal, do not kill, and so on—not just because of their convenience to society, but because we know they have a power and an authority over us and we cannot resist them once we recognize they exist.

Finally, however, Socrates says that the lover will be led to the Good, which is the highest principle of all and absolute Beauty in itself. The Good is the source of all spiritual life and it cannot be resisted. Indeed, the closer we come to the Good, the more it empowers us, and the more we are transformed by it. In fact, we become filled with the power of goodness, and so *we* become good. In this way, we reach our spiritual goal, after a long journey that began with the love of individual beauty. But now we understand that it was goodness that inspired us all along, and goodness that we were looking for; we just had not known it until that moment:

> And if . . . man's life is ever worth the living, it is when he has attained this vision of the very soul of beauty. And once you have seen it, you will never be seduced again by the charm of gold . . . you will care nothing for the beauties that used to take your breath away and kindle such a longing in you, and many others like you . . . But if it were given to man to gaze on beauty's very self—unsullied, unalloyed, and freed from the mortal taint that haunts the frailer loveliness of flesh and blood—if, I say, it were given to man to see the heavenly beauty face to face, would you call *his* . . . an unenviable life, whose eyes had been opened to the vision, and who had gazed upon it in true contemplation until it had become his own forever?[15]

As Socrates points out, this is not an intellectual quest where we finally get to *understand* the meaning of life. It is a spiritual quest that starts with a sense of wonder—the shock of beauty that pulls us away from our self and our everyday concerns—and it ends with spiritual fulfillment. Of course, all of this is just a speech in praise of love; it is a philosophical story whose meaning may resonate with us, even if it is hard to explain exactly what is

15. Plato, *Symposium*, 211e.

being described. But Plato's account remains compelling because it makes sense of mindfulness and wonder, and it helps us to understand why they are so important in the progress of our spiritual lives.

All in all, life is inherently mysterious and magical, and openness to this mystery is a key to spiritual experience. The psychologist Carl Jung expresses this basic spiritual attitude in his autobiography, which is called *Memories, Dreams, Reflections*. Toward the close of this book, he describes his position in a remarkable passage that encapsulates much of what we have sought to affirm in this chapter: "It is important to have a secret," he writes, and,

> a premonition of things unknown. It fills life with something im-
> personal, a *numinosum*. A man who has never experienced that
> has missed something important. He must sense that he lives in
> a world which in some respects is mysterious; that things happen
> and can be experienced which remain inexplicable; that not ev-
> erything which happens can be anticipated. The unexpected and
> the incredible belong in this world. Only then is life whole. For me
> the world has from the beginning been infinite and ungraspable.[16]

Like Mojud in the Sufi story, Jung felt the mystery of life as something that must be experienced, but not as a mystery that has to be solved.

The third step of enlightenment involves cultivating mindfulness and wonder, which includes a sense of attunement to the ordinary and extraordinary miracles of life, such as love and nature, art, truth and beauty. Meditation and prayer can promote mindfulness and a sense of wonder, and they cut through our routine experience of the world to reveal the sacred dimension of life, which is always there, even though it may be hidden from view. Typically, we are only aware of the "routine world" because we lack a spiritual imagination; but the latter is something that love and other miracles can inspire within us now. And so we must live in mindfulness and wonder, for without these things the world is never more than an ordinary place, and we will resemble the *prisoners* that Plato describes at the lowest level of reality in the Cave of everyday life.

---

16. Jung, *Memories, Dreams, Reflections*, 356.

5

Accepting Death and Returning to Joy

HOW SHOULD WE THINK about death and dying? We spend all of our lives building relationships and families; we study hard in school, we fall in love, and we devote ourselves to different careers and interests, but in the end, it all comes to nothing, as death undermines everything that we have created for ourselves. People say that nothing lasts forever, and this is certainly true of our individual existence here on earth. But does this mean that death takes away meaning? Or could death be a more significant aspect of our spiritual existence, and a part of the meaning of our lives?

At the beginning of this book, I talked about my life as a philosopher. In recent times a lot of philosophical writing has become quite technical, and many philosophers have simply lost touch with what should be most important. But if you go back to the beginning of Western thought, in ancient Greece and Rome, the whole point of philosophy was to teach people how to live in the right way. For the ancient philosophers, philosophy was a kind of medicine that was supposed to cure the ailments of the soul, and this meant living well and cultivating the proper attitude towards adversity, sickness, and death. I have always been drawn to philosophical reflections on death and dying, and I think the first philosophers have a lot to teach us about how to live our lives in the face of our mortality. We are limited beings because one day we will die. But this does not make our lives pointless in the end. Nor does it mean that in the long run it really doesn't matter what we do. Philosophy can help us to live a spiritual life in spite of the challenges that we face. And this includes death—not only our own death, of course, but the death of others, our friends and our loved ones, which can destroy the very fabric of our lives and make all of our normal activities feel pointless and absurd.

Socrates said that philosophy is a preparation for death and dying, and the writer Montaigne put the same point even more succinctly when he wrote that: "To study philosophy is to learn how to die."[1] This implies that there is a right way and a wrong way of dealing with death and its place in our lives. And the proper attitude to death, even if it doesn't come naturally, is something we must learn to cultivate within ourselves. Many, if not most of us are afraid of death and dying. We enjoy our lives, and it is only "natural" to think of death as a bad thing because it means the end of everything that we enjoy. And so we don't want to think about death; and even though we know that we must die one day, this is not something that we dwell on. In the midst of our life projects and goals, we act as if we were immortal. The fact that we are going to die at some point, whether five, ten, or fifty years from now, does not seem to make the slightest bit of difference to the way that we live now.

I am not going to discuss religious beliefs or the possibility of personal immortality in this chapter. Socrates wisely said that *no one* knows what happens when we die; death may be annihilation, which is like a long dreamless sleep, or when we die we may find ourselves in a different realm of being, which could be something like heaven.[2] But in either case, death is not something that we should be afraid of. We may have faith or remain skeptical of all religious possibilities, but in the end we just don't know; indeed, we cannot *know*, and this is exactly why religious beliefs are matters of *faith* rather than knowledge. Like everyone else, I have my own ideas about personal immortality and God, but I have noticed that these ideas have changed over the course of time, and I think they may continue to evolve. People lose their faith, and even atheists have deathbed conversions. The point that I want to make here is that life can have spiritual significance regardless of whether God exists and regardless of whether there is or there isn't any life after death. For once we can accept death, we are free to experience the fullness of life.

1. See Plato's discussion of death in the *Phaedo*, 64a; also, Montaigne's essay on the same theme, "That to Philosophize is to Learn to Die" in Montaigne, *The Complete Essays of Montaigne*, 56-68.

2. Plato, *Apology* 40c–e.

Death and the Individual: The Case of Ivan Ilych

Death is often treated as the enemy, and the absolute negation of life itself. But death is a part of life, and since everything that lives is continually in the process of dying, I think a more spiritual response would be to look at life and death as two sides of the same coin. From which it follows that avoiding the reality of death is not a spiritual attitude. Indeed it can be spiritually disastrous if we spend our lives engaged in selfish or trivial pursuits, because at some point, when death becomes unavoidable, we will realize how much we have squandered by focusing our attention on things that are really not so important. One famous example in modern literature is Tolstoy's short novel, *The Death of Ivan Ilych*. Ivan Ilych was a man who spent his whole life trying to be a good civil servant. He always did what was expected of him. He married and had a family just because this was the expected thing to do. He was a dutiful parent and husband, but he never really cared about anything except his own personal success and advancement. He spent a lot of time playing cards and going to fashionable balls and parties. One day, when he was finishing the decoration of his new apartment, and feeling completely satisfied with himself, Ivan fell while he was hanging up a curtain. Tolstoy tells us that from this point on, Ivan became sick. He had injured something inside himself, and as he became sicker, the life that he had been living became completely abhorrent to him. It soon becomes clear that he is going to die, but he stubbornly refuses to face the reality of his own demise. On the one hand, he cannot bring himself to accept the fact that he is going to die because he seems to think of death as an abstraction that applies to other people rather than himself. As Tolstoy puts it:

> In the depth of his heart he knew that he was dying, but not only was he not accustomed to the thought, he simply did not and could not grasp it.
>
> The syllogism he had learnt from Kiezewetter's Logic: "Caius is a man, men are mortal, therefore Caius is mortal," had always seemed to him correct as applied to Caius, but certainly not as applied to himself. That Caius—man in the abstract—was mortal, was perfectly correct, but he was not Caius, not an abstract man, but a creature quite different, quite separate from all others . . . "Caius really was mortal and it was right for him to die; but for me, little Vanya, Ivan Ilych, with all my thoughts and emotions, it's altogether a different matter. It cannot be that I ought to die. That would be too terrible."[3]

3. Tolstoy, *The Death of Ivan Ilych, and Other Stories*, 131–32.

At the same time, Ivan doesn't think that he has ever done anything to deserve what is happening to him now, and so he concludes that *it can't be happening*:

> "Maybe I did not live as I ought to have done," it suddenly occurred to him. "But how could that be, when I did everything properly?" he replied, and immediately dismissed from his mind this, the sole solution of all the riddles of life and death, as something quite impossible.[4]

Finally, though, towards the very end of his life, and in a state of delirium, he experiences a surge of compassion for others, and immediately he has a feeling of spiritual release. His pain and mental anguish seem to disappear and he feels at one with the world:

> He asked himself, "What is the right thing?" and grew still, listening. Then he felt that someone was kissing his hand. He opened his eyes, looked at his son, and felt sorry for him. His wife came up to him and he glanced at her. She was gazing at him open-mouthed, with undried tears on her face. He felt sorry for her too . . . And suddenly it grew clear to him that what had been oppressing him and would not leave him was all dropping away at once from two sides, from ten sides, and from all sides. He was sorry for them, he must act so as not to hurt them: release them and free himself from these sufferings. "How good and how simple!" he thought. "and the pain?" he asked himself. "What has become of it? Where are you, pain?"[5]

Ivan understands that he has not lived his life in the right way. He was preoccupied with material success and avoided spiritual values. But when he accepts the fact that he is going to die, he experiences a kind of spiritual peace for perhaps the first time in his life.

The Death of Ivan Ilych is an astonishing book, and like most of Tolstoy's writings it is full of spiritual insights. I think we are all a bit like Ivan at some point in our lives. We allow ourselves to be distracted from what is most important—which means living a spiritual life and cultivating spiritual values that will bring us more deeply into life itself—and we lose ourselves in the pursuit of popularity, money and power. In this way, *The Death of Ivan Ilych* speaks to all of us both as a reminder and as a warning. The interesting thing is that Ivan only comes back to himself once he realizes

4. Ibid., 148.
5. Ibid., 155.

that he is going to die at some time in the not too distant future. But instead of making his life meaningless, the realization of his own mortality gives Ivan a sense of spiritual meaning and significance even though he only achieves this right at the very end. This is tragic in its own way; but the underlying point is that the life that he lived until then was spiritually empty, and only by facing up to death does he experience a spiritual awakening. Hence, Ivan's final words: "Death is finished . . . It is no more"—are not so paradoxical.[6] Of course, these words may reflect Tolstoy's strong religious faith, but they also seem to emphasize the "death" or spiritual oblivion of Ivan's own life, which is finally coming to an end.

Now let's bring all of this back to Socrates: When Socrates says that philosophy is "a preparation for dying," he means that through philosophical reflection we can come to know ourselves, we can come to terms with the fact that we are mortal and only have a limited understanding of the world; and this allows us to put our lives in a proper perspective. The point is not to run away from death but to face up to it—for the fact of death creates a focus that life would never have if it lasted forever. In this respect, death has a spiritual significance, because death—either the death of someone that we know or the anticipation of our own death—calls us back to ourselves and forces us to come to terms with the spiritual reality of our lives. So we must think about death and keep the possibility of our own death before us. Without becoming obsessive, we must ask ourselves: How do we really want to live our lives? What is most important for us? And what would we like to be remembered for?

Philosophy and Death

But if we are afraid of death, how can we ever gain a more positive attitude towards it? I think that philosophy can help us to answer this question, and in the rest of this chapter I will look at three arguments from classical philosophy and one story from ancient Chinese thought. Philosophers can make sense of difficult spiritual questions, and using rational reflection they can free us from ordinary ways of thinking so that we can make spiritual progress. On the face of it, it seems obvious that death is a bad thing because we usually try to avoid it, and the death of the people that we love can ruin our lives. But at the same time, death is good insofar as it gives us

6. Ibid., 156.

a spiritual compass and an urgent or heightened sense of life; and perhaps there are other ways death can provide us with meaning.

First, Epicurus, one of the early Greek philosophers says that "death is nothing to us." Why? Because while we are alive death is not present, and so it cannot affect us; but when we are dead, we no longer exist, and so we cannot be *hurt* by death or by anything else. His actual words are as follows:

> So death, the most terrifying of ills, is nothing to us, since so long as we exist, death is nothing with us; but when death comes, then we do not exist. It does not then concern either the living or the dead, since for the former it is not, and the latter are no more.[7]

Perhaps this is true in the same sense that when we are asleep we *usually* aren't bothered by the things we have to deal with in our waking lives, and when we are awake we are not preoccupied with our dreams. Epicurus is saying death does not matter to us; and so we shouldn't fear death. This seems very philosophical, but it's not entirely convincing. What is so bad about death or being dead? Epicurus would say that unlike physical pain, public humiliation, romantic breakups, or any other things that we may be afraid of, we don't experience our own death. Death is not just another event in life. To be more precise, it is not something that happens *to us* since it is the end of the self as we know it. So how can it be bad for a person to be dead, because that person isn't even there anymore! Even so, this is not a very satisfying argument because right now we *are* afraid of what might happen in the future when we die. The whole point is that we *don't know* if death is the end or not, and our ignorance about death doesn't allow us to rest easy. Will we be reunited with our loved ones when we die? Will we go to heaven or will we be extinguished? We just don't know; and to say that when we die we won't be able to worry about such things is not that comforting to us now. Perhaps this is just another way of saying that "what you don't know can't hurt you"; but if it is, I don't think the argument is very convincing. For one thing, I *can* be hurt by what other people say about me, and my reputation will suffer even if I never find out that other people have talked about me behind my back. Likewise, it really matters to me to *know* that my spouse or my children love me, and I would still be "betrayed" even if I never find out that they don't care for me. Of course, Epicurus would simply reply that if I am dead I can't be hurt by anything, because *I* am no longer there to be affected by anything at all!

7. Epicurus, "Letter to Menoeceus," 31.

It is likely that Epicurus didn't want people to worry about all the terrors that are sometimes associated with the afterlife, including hell and eternal punishment for one's crimes. Now many of us would still fear death even if we *knew* that death was simply annihilation; and it does not seem obvious that this fear is completely unreasonable. Even so, I think he is trying to offer us some comfort: So much of our time is spent worrying about ourselves and the future and worrying about death. Epicurus is raising the idea that death represents an end to all anxieties, when we really will be at peace. This may not calm all of our fears, but it frames death more positively as a release from suffering, "eternal rest," or the peace that passes all understanding. And this is not a terrible thing.

The Roman philosopher and poet Lucretius was a great admirer of Epicurus, and in his poem *On the Nature of the Universe*, he praises Epicurus while he reaffirms the view that death is completely irrelevant to us. Lucretius then goes on to offer two additional arguments for why it would be wrong to fear death. First, he points out that death is just a part of nature, and that nature is basically *good*. In fact he imagines what "Nature" would say if she could speak to us about our foolish resistance to dying, since dying is a very *natural* process:

> Suppose that Nature herself were suddenly to find a voice and round upon us in one of these terms: "What is your grievance, mortal, that you give yourself up to this whining and repining? Why do you weep and wail over death? If the life you have lived till now has been a pleasant thing—if all its blessings have not leaked away like water poured into a cracked pot and run to waste unrelished—why then, you silly creature, do you not retire as a guest who has had his fill of life and take your care-free rest with a quiet mind. Or, if all your gains have been poured profitless away and life has grown distasteful, why do you seek to swell the total? The new can but turn out as badly as the old and perish as unprofitably . . . Have done with your grumbling! You are withering now after tasting all the joys of life. But because you are always pining for what is not and unappreciative of the things at hand, your life has slipped away unfulfilled and unprized . . . The old is always thrust aside to make way for the new, and one thing must be built on the wreck of another . . . Bygone generations have taken your road, and those to come will take it no less. So one thing will never cease to spring from another."[8]

8. Lucretius, *On the Nature of the Universe*, 90–91.

The seasons come and go. Plants and animals live their lives and then they are replaced by others just like them. But it is exactly the same with human beings. We are born, we grow up and flourish, and then we decline and die. The next generation succeeds us, and the whole thing happens all over again. This is just the stream of life and the way things are. Each individual death is a part of life, and it wouldn't be in the order of things if we lived forever. So in the end, to accept death is to be well-adjusted to nature; while to fear death is to be out of attunement with everything.

There are two points that we need to think about here. The first point is that death is something natural, and so it is not an objection to life. But then there is also the problem of a premature death, which could be "tragic" even if death in the ordinary course of nature—a timely death—is not considered tragic but only sad. The first point seems right to me: In Western culture we have become used to thinking in terms of the absolute value of the individual, and we don't focus as much as we should on our sense of belonging to a larger group—the family, humankind, or the stream of life itself. But we can often find meaning through a sense of belonging to something that is much greater than ourselves. You may die in the cause of freedom; but if you have the hope that one day your cause will triumph, then you may not think that your sacrifice is in vain. Likewise, the sense of belonging to humanity or nature can inspire you with a sense of being an integral part of the whole that will continue long after you are gone, and perhaps indefinitely. It is significant that in recent years we have become much more concerned about the fate of future generations and what we owe to them. Such people have not even been born yet, but there seems to be growing agreement that we should leave a sustainable world to all those who come after us. We should not pollute the world or deplete the earth's resources because we are a part of humankind, and we owe it to those who will live their lives after we are gone to be mindful of what we are doing now. This is why it would be terrible to find out that shortly after our own death an asteroid or a plague was going to destroy all life on earth! For even though we would not be around to experience such a cataclysm, we would still be distraught because we think of ourselves as a part of the greater whole that is humanity (or even just Nature itself).[9] So our own death may not be so terrible if we know that the stream of life will continue after we are gone.

9. For a much fuller discussion of this kind of thought experiment, see Scheffler, *Death and the Afterlife*.

But what about the other point, that death can be premature? In an obvious sense, it would be tragic to die before you have experienced many of life's possibilities. Think about the promising student who dies in a senseless accident before she is able to make any contribution to the world; the Romantic poet John Keats, who died of tuberculosis at the age of twenty-five; or the ten-year-old boy with a brain tumor who only wanted to read Charles Dickens's novel *The Pickwick Papers*, but who died before he could finish the book. We say that such cases are "tragic" because the individuals involved did not realize their full potential. But the fact is, people often die before they are truly ready to die, and there is always "more to do." And like the young leaves that get torn off a tree during a storm, this is *also* a part of nature. We cannot change what has happened, but we can learn to be thankful for the gift of the child, the parent, the brother, or the sister that we have lost; and as I will explain, we can still affirm their lives as an integral part of the cosmos itself. The tragedy—if there is a tragedy—is not to die young, but to die without having lived a meaningful life.

Lucretius's second argument is also provocative:

> Look back at the eternity that passed before we were born, and mark how utterly it counts to us as nothing. This is a mirror that Nature holds up to us, in which we may see the time that shall be after we are dead. Is there anything terrifying in the sight— anything depressing—anything that is not more restful than the soundest sleep?[10]

According to Lucretius, the time that existed before our birth is exactly similar to the time that will exist after our death. But then he says, if we are not dismayed by our own nonexistence in the past, there is no reason to be upset by our own nonexistence in the future, for the two times are exactly the same. This is an interesting idea, but the typical response to it tells us something very important about human nature. Maybe we are *not* upset that we weren't around for the Declaration of Independence or when the first man landed on the moon; but our *future* nonbeing is of much more concern to us, because we are future-oriented beings. As human beings, we care about the success of our individual projects and the continued well-being of our loved ones; we want to be with those that we care about in the future, and so we don't want our lives to come to an end. There is nothing that we can call ours that existed in the past before we were born, but the

10. Ibid., 82.

things that we have now—our own projects, our friends and family—are *not* things that we want to be cut off from.

So on the face of it this is not such a good argument because these two times—the time before our birth and the time after our death—are not really parallel to each other. Once again, however, I think the discussion remains helpful for at least two reasons. First, if you are afraid of dying and you contemplate your future nonexistence with dread, you should remember that you already "know" what this nonexistence is like because you didn't exist before you were born, and realizing this is something that can help you to cope now. The other reason is that it forces us to think about our place in the cosmos. However long we live—one year, ten years or a hundred years—our existence is just a short moment in the life of the universe itself. There was an infinite time before we were born, and there will be an infinite time after we are gone. We are usually limited by our own narrow perspective on life, and we focus on our ego. But we can also try to contemplate the universe as a whole. For example, imagine yourself going up into space and looking down at your house, and then looking down on your street, going higher still you look down on your town, your country, and eventually the earth itself. Then, going even higher, imagine looking down on the planets and finally the universe from your vantage point beyond the cosmos. In this way, you can shift your perspective to grasp the minuteness of your own existence and the insignificance of your life when compared to the entirety of everything that is. But at the same time, such imaginative visualization also inspires a sense of belonging—rather than alienation—that makes you feel a significant part of the universe itself. In the words of the poet Rilke, who sought to articulate these things:

> Being here is so much, because
> everything in this fleeting world seems to need us
> and strangely concerns us. Us, the most fleeting of all.
> Each thing once. One time and never again. And we too,
> just once. And yet to have existed once,
> even if only once, and to have been a part
> of this earth—this cannot be undone.[11]

---

11. The quotation is from Rilke, *Duino Elegies*: "The Ninth Elegy," my own translation. There are many translations of the *Duino Elegies*, including a helpful bilingual edition with translation by Edward Snow.

This is the experience of our own unique and unrepeatable existence, and this is impressed upon us in the deepest moments of life, when we are called back to ourselves. Somehow we must balance this perspective, which is intensely personal, with the big picture of the universe or the cosmos itself, in which we play a much smaller part. *Both* perspectives are essential, and as we will see, this helps us to think about the ultimate relationship between life and death, the self and the universe we belong to.

Death and Mourning

Epicurus and Lucretius help us to think more clearly about death; and they challenge the almost universal fear of death, by suggesting some ways in which death is not as terrible as we might have thought it was. Their arguments are very brief and condensed, and we can think of them as "spiritual exercises" that we can continually return to and mull. To bring some of these ideas about death into clearer focus, we can also think about another story from a very different cultural tradition: In the Chinese classic *The Book of Chuang Tzu* there is a story about the Chinese sage, Chuang Tzu, who is associated with the philosophy of Daoism. Chuang Tzu's wife has died, and his friend Hui Tzu comes to console him. But when he arrives, he finds Chuang Tzu sitting, legs akimbo, beating on a battered old tub and singing loudly. Hui Tzu is shocked at his friend's behavior, and so he remonstrates with Chuang Tzu: "She was your wife; she raised your children; after death you should be weeping, rather than banging on a tub and singing. This is not right affirmation."[12] Chuang Tzu replies that when she first died, he mourned like anyone else. But then he thought back to her birth and "the very roots of being," even before she was born. "Indeed," he continues:

> not just before she was born but before the time when her body was created. Not just before her body was created but before the very origin of her life's breath. Out of all this, through the wonderful mystery of change she was given her life's breath. Her life's breath wrought a transformation and she had a body. Her body wrought a transformation and she was born. Now there is yet another transformation and she is dead. She is like the four seasons in the way that spring, summer, autumn and winter follow each other. She is now at peace, lying in her chamber, but if I were to sob

12. Chuang Tzu, *The Book of Chuang Tzu*, 151.

and cry it would certainly appear that I could not comprehend the ways of destiny. This is why I stopped.[13]

In this passage, Chuang Tzu tells Hui Tzu that he has already mourned for the wife that he loved. But after his initial grief he came to realize that her life was just a part of the totality of the universe, and the destiny that rules the world. And this is something that he must embrace. It is not that everything always happens for a good reason, or as some people say, "everything is always for the best." He is not saying that the world is reasonable and that his wife's death is somehow a good thing. But rather he is saying that beyond his own personal grief—which is also an essential part of the world and cannot be diminished—the world has a larger reality, and after the first shock of his wife's passing, he is bound to experience her death as part of the mystery of life itself. He cannot explain it, he can only sing a song of praise while beating on his tub, because nature and the world are good.

Now I think that this is a very spiritual response to the problem of death that challenges the meaning of our lives. In some religious and spiritual traditions we are told not to form strong attachments, because everything must pass away, and if we make a strong emotional bond, we are bound to suffer distress at some point because people leave: they can abandon us, and eventually they will die. Typically, in any relationship, one person must die before the other one, and this means that the survivor must deal with grief that can ruin the rest of her life. So it is held that we can never achieve happiness or equanimity in life for as long as we make ourselves dependent on other people or things that are beyond our control—and this includes falling in love or caring deeply for our family or our friends. The Stoics think along these lines when they charge us to cultivate indifference to whatever happens: "If you kiss your child or your wife," Epictetus says, "say that you are kissing a human being, for when it dies you will not be upset."[14] Buddhism also urges nonattachment as the key to equanimity. In Christianity the love of other people has sometimes been seen as an obstacle to the love of God. For how can we really love God if we are madly in love with another human being?

The problem with this kind of thinking is that we are being asked to reject something—love, in the sense of a strong personal attachment—which is one of life's greatest pleasures and the source of personal fulfillment. Love is also a spiritual catalyst, as Socrates argued in the *Symposium*, and without

13. Ibid., 162–63.
14. Epictetus, *Handbook*, 3, 12.

it we could not experience the underlying mystery of the world. Obviously, certain kinds of attachment can be harmful and excessive, but should we really abandon all forms of love simply because they *can* lead to heartbreak or disappointment when the loved one leaves us or dies? To live without love is to live without something that seems to make life worth living. And it is not clear that a loveless life would be preferable even with all the dangers that attachment may bring.

Now there are some problems associated with mourning, and the anguish that the death of others can cause us is profound. We might even ask ourselves, *why* do we mourn? Do we owe it to the dead? But the dead are gone; they have ceased to exist or perhaps they exist in another place, but in either case they will not return. So they do not need our mourning or our compassion. Sometimes we say, "If he was here with us today," but the point is he is *not* here. We have lost him, and we are lost without him, and so it seems that we must be grieving for ourselves and for our own situation. Sometimes people say, "I am sorry for *your* loss." But this is not right either, because it makes the survivor, rather than the departed, into the central figure. And if the goal is just to get over our *own* pain, then we must eventually abandon the departed whom we claim to love, and this would be like killing him for a second time. So why do we mourn? Obviously, mourning helps us to get over the pain of our loss; but from one perspective it seems like a betrayal: It appears that hanging on and letting go are both inappropriate responses to bereavement, so what are we to do?

In fact, the story about Chuang Tzu gives us a very good model for thinking about our spiritual relationship to death and mourning. Chuang Tzu loved his wife, and he mourned her in the appropriate ways. But eventually he was able to understand her life as a part of something greater, and so he sang a song of praise to nature that had given her to him in the first place. Her life—like our own life—didn't just come into the world but came out of it; it belonged to it, and it was ultimately an expression of the whole of life (or "nature") itself. So there are two perspectives here—the personal perspective of Chuang Tzu, who loved his wife and mourned her loss, and the cosmological perspective in which every death is an event in relation to the whole. The key is to honor *both* perspectives, and this is exactly what Chuang Tzu does. He does not retreat from life; and he doesn't bear his loss with a sense of despair that suggests that he will never be able to enjoy his life again. He accepts death, but at the same time he returns to joy as he beats on his tub with delighted exuberance. But this is not a strange aberration. In everyday life people celebrate the life of one who has departed; and they are often able to find meaning in a personal tragedy by using the death of another to create something that is inherently good. In this way it is also possible to revalue the meaning of death and dying.

Take the case of Matthew Shepard, for example. Matthew was a twenty-one-year-old student at the University of Wyoming. He was gay, and in October 1998 he was murdered by two local men who lured him from a bar, robbed him, beat him with a pistol and then left him tied to a fence on a windswept prairie. He was not discovered for eighteen hours and he died several days later in a hospital, having never regained consciousness. His parents were devastated, but they were able to create meaning out of this tragedy. First, they interceded to save the lives of Matthew's killers. Citing Matthew's special gift for helping people, his father was able to overcome his own desire for revenge; and in court he addressed his son's killers: "This is the time to begin the healing process. To show mercy to someone who refused to show any mercy . . . I am going to grant you life, as hard as it is for me to do so, because of Matthew."[15] The Shepards went on to create the Matthew Shepard Foundation to honor Matthew's life, and to continue his passion of fostering a more just and caring world. The explicit goal of the foundation is "to erase hate by replacing it with understanding, compassion and acceptance."[16] The foundation helped to pioneer important hate-crime legislation, most notably the Matthew Shepard and James E. Byrd Jr. Hate Crime Prevention Act of 2009, which made it a federal crime to assault someone because of their sexual orientation or gender identity; and the foundation continues to sponsor programs that create dialogue and acceptance. But this is by no means an isolated example. There are many cases like this, even if most of them are not quite as dramatic as this one. The underlying point of the story is how the Shepards loved their son, they accepted his death and mourned him; but at the same time they did not abandon life by retreating into despair. They forgave their son's killers, and they used his death to create something good. This was a truly spiritual response to death, but it was based on love and "attachment" rather than the avoidance of desire, which can never lead to spiritual overcoming. Once again, something like this may be the best model for thinking about death

15. The speech is given verbatim in Moisés Kaufmann's play about this case, *The Laramie Project*, 96.

16. This is part of the mission statement of the Matthew Shepard Foundation: www. matthewshepard.org.

and mourning, for it expresses joy at the life of the departed; and those who benefit from the foundation's programs are likely to benefit others so that the gift of Matthew's life will continue.

The philosophers that we talked about earlier—Socrates, Epicurus, Lucretius, and Chuang Tzu—were very much aware that we should be ready to die at any moment. And the Sufi master Rumi was fond of repeating the same instruction: "You must die before you die!"[17] He meant that we are only ready to die once we have abandoned all of our selfish, personal desires, and live for the sake of spiritual perfection. In many religious and spiritual traditions—Buddhism, Christianity and Hinduism, for example— true spiritual enlightenment involves the death of the ordinary ego or the separate self, that plots its own advancement and enjoyment, and when this happens we are complete and "ready to die" in the original Socratic sense. For now we have achieved an authentic spiritual life and the goal of our quest, and we are ready to face whatever might come next.

The Importance of Joy

Clearly our attitude towards death is of great spiritual significance. And I think it goes without saying that we cannot allow the fear of death and personal extinction to cast such a shadow over our lives that we retreat into dejection or the avoidance of life altogether. The spiritual goal is to accept death as a part of life that allows us to be who we are—mindful beings with a strong sense of spiritual purpose and compassion for others. But we must also stay open for joy, which is the pure celebration of life and being in this world. Joy is not just foolish exuberance. It is difficult to articulate these things, and sometimes we seem to lack the spiritual vocabulary for it. But the experience of joy is important because it reflects a sense of belonging to *this* life as something that is inherently good, even if it does not last forever.

Very few writers have been able to capture the experience of joy in a convincing or compelling way, but perhaps the philosopher Jean-Jacques Rousseau comes close. Towards the end of his life he spent hours walking every day, reflecting on the life that he had lived and trying to make sense of it all. He transcribed these meditations into a notebook, from which the *Reveries of the Solitary Walker* was published after his death. In this work, he describes joy as the pure experience of being, which is unencumbered by any personal desires or goals:

17. See for example, Rumi, *The Mathnawi*, vol. 3: "Die before ye die," 298–301.

But if there is a state where the soul can find a resting-place secure enough to establish itself and concentrate its entire being there, with no need to remember the past or reach into the future, where time is nothing to it, where the present runs on indefinitely but this duration goes unnoticed, with no sign of the passing of time, and no other feeling of deprivation or enjoyment, pleasure or pain, desire or fear than the simple feeling of existence, a feeling that fills our soul entirely, as long as this state lasts, we can call ourselves happy, not with the poor, incomplete and relative happiness, such as we find in the pleasures of life, but with a sufficient, complete and perfect happiness, which leaves no emptiness to be filled in the soul.[18]

Joy is a special kind of emotion that affirms and discloses the spiritual character of the world to us. It implies self-overcoming, and the feeling of complete presence, or being absolutely here and now. Such "perfect happiness" involves the affirmation of life; and in this respect it is also an expression of spiritual fulfillment.

Rousseau asks: "What is the source of our happiness in such a state?" And he answers:

Nothing external to us, nothing apart from ourselves and our own existence; as long as this state lasts we are self-sufficient like God. The feeling of existence unmixed with any other emotion is in itself a precious feeling of peace and contentment which would be enough to make this mode of being loved and cherished by anyone who could guard against all the earthly and sensual influences that are constantly distracting us from it in this life and troubling the joy it could give us.[19]

Rousseau points out that this is not really a *personal* experience or a feeling of selfish pleasure. In fact, it is defined by the absence of personal longing. More positively, it is a *disinterested* feeling of joy which affirms the existence of the world and our sense of belonging to it. It is the celebration of life and all that we have been given to enjoy—now, and at this very moment! For here, we experience ourselves as an integral part of the cosmos; our joy includes a profound gratitude for what we have been given; and it leads us to open our hearts to all living beings.

Perhaps we can remember having had such an experience in our own life—where everything was suddenly perfect. We may describe it differently,

18. Rousseau, *Reveries of the Solitary Walker*, 88.

19. Ibid., 89.

as a kind of happiness, tranquility, or bliss, and we may need to understand it from a religious perspective as the direct experience of God. But regardless of how we describe it, it is an exceptional experience in which we feel completely at one or at peace with ultimate reality, however this is finally understood. And this is one thing that allows us to feel at peace with death. By contrast, some other perspectives encourage us to cope with death by shutting down our desires and affections and by keeping a safe distance from all the good things in life, including love. But we can only affirm life and be spiritually fulfilled if we can accept death *and* stay open for joy. And this is the ultimate spiritual challenge. The proximity of our own death casts a shadow over the life we are living now; and the death of those we love can be unendurable. But we *can* return to joy, and we must remain open to its recovery, even if this seems impossible to us now. Certainly, the most spiritually enlightened people are often the most joyful and happy ones we know, for in spite of all the troubles and tragedies they face, they can still see the goodness of life and they can affirm its spiritual depth. They have not abandoned this life by retreating into despair and misery, even if suffering and death have been a big part of their lives.

There is a well known parable from the Zen Buddhist tradition that perfectly describes how life can still be cherished in spite of its apparent limitations and the inevitability of dying:

> A man traveling across a field encountered a tiger. He fled, the tiger after him. Coming to a precipice, he caught hold of the root of a wild vine and swung himself down over the edge. The tiger sniffed at him from above. Trembling, the man looked down to where, far below, another tiger was waiting to eat him. Only the vine sustained him.
>
> Two mice, one white and one black, little by little started to gnaw away the vine. The man saw a luscious strawberry near him. Grasping the vine with one hand, he plucked the strawberry with the other. How sweet it tasted.[20]

The parable tells us that life is inherently valuable. The strawberry tastes so good! It can be relished and enjoyed, but eventually something will happen to end this impossible situation because life is fragile, and everything is bound to pass away. Should we be afraid? No. And I think the more well-disposed toward life we are, the more we can view death as a natural end and as a kind of fulfillment. Fear of death is a measure of how much

20. Reps and Senzaki, compilers, *Zen Flesh, Zen Bones*, 38–39.

spiritual progress we still have to make; for spiritual flourishing and the acceptance of death must ultimately go together.

The fourth step on the path of enlightenment involves accepting death and returning to joy. But this is never easy, for the death of one we love can completely undermine our sense of who we are, and in contemplating our own death we can be plunged into despair. Usually we think of death as the enemy, or as the opposite of life. But death is actually a part of life—this is what nature tells us—and our own existence will be spiritually diminished unless we can learn to accept life-and-death as one complete whole, or as two sides of the same coin. There is a mystery here that many have tried to understand, but the bottom line is that life and death go together. We must learn to affirm both the individual and the cosmological perspectives because they are equal conditions for living a spiritual life. We must practice coming to terms with death and be ready to die at every moment, and in this way we can return to joy—for joy is the fulfillment of spiritual life in which we identify most completely with the goodness of the world. And even though it may seem *obvious* that life is preferable to death, in the end we cannot take even this much for granted. As Socrates comments with wisdom and great humility immediately after he has been sentenced to death: "The hour of departure has arrived, and we go our ways—I to die and you to live. Which is better God only knows."[21] Death is a mystery that cannot be solved now. At the same time, it must be said that a spiritual life involves a basic trust in the generosity of this world, and the sense that life must be celebrated rather than rejected or disdained.

21. Plato, *Apology* 42a.

6

Conclusion

AT THE BEGINNING OF this book I talked about my own experience as a philosopher. Philosophy can be a very critical discipline, and the emphasis on argument and critical thinking can undermine spiritual beliefs. But not everything is rational, and there are some aspects of life—including art or love—which cannot be reduced to reasons or concepts although they have a powerful hold on us. Beethoven's Fifth Symphony, Shakespeare's *Hamlet*, Leonardo da Vinci's *Mona Lisa*, and many other works of art have a tremendous effect upon listeners or viewers, but this effect cannot easily be put into words or explained in terms of ideas. The same thing is true of spirituality. You cannot reduce spirituality to a set of ideas, and any attempt to limit it to this rational level is in some sense to destroy it.

Spirituality is wisdom that we can live by. Not just knowledge or information that helps us to deal with practical problems, but an authentic understanding of the world that can be incorporated into the deepest level of who we are. A spiritually wise person is someone who has a sense of what is really important, and what isn't. He or she will know how to deal with problems that arise in the course of life; they will also have a sense of the big picture and how to remain focused on matters of ultimate concern. One traditional way of communicating wisdom is through stories—like Plato's story of the Cave and the incredible life of Mojud, the legend of Job, the death of Ivan Ilych, and all the stories of forgiveness we have encountered in this book. Information requires passive acceptance, but a story is a narrative that requires activity on the part of the readers or listeners to make sense of things by incorporating the meaning of the story into the context of their lives. This is why many of the great teachers of the world, such as

Jesus or Buddha, have used parables and stories to impart their wisdom. Today storytelling may be in decline because we rely on prepackaged information—newspapers, television, the Internet—which requires no effort on our part. But by returning to significant stories and paying attention to them, we can glimpse the possibility of wisdom that can lead us towards the truth. For storytelling is one source of our collective wisdom.

In addition to stories, philosophy can also help us come to grips with spiritual matters. Spirituality is an ambiguous field that is hard to put into words; but there is a very close relationship between spirituality and philosophy because both of them are concerned with the nature of ultimate reality and meaning. It needs to be emphasized, though, that philosophy is all about *thinking for yourself*. The early philosophers questioned many of the rules and the beliefs of those who supported religion—not for the sake of causing trouble, but because they thought that any important claim must be defended and argued for. And I am asking *you* to think for yourself. Don't accept everything that you read (including this book), and don't believe everything that you are told! Reflect on what you have been told; ask yourself whether it sounds reasonable or not, and whether it conforms to your own experience of the world. Go to lectures and presentations, listen to people who seem to have lives that are spiritually full, and talk to spiritual advisers. And always *read* more, so that you can learn more about the different spiritual traditions. Some people make fun of spirituality, and the "spiritual shopping" that seems to go on, and they say that spirituality is one more field that has been commodified by capitalism. But another way of thinking about this is just to acknowledge that through the Internet, all the different courses given at different spiritual centers, and the huge number of spiritual books that are currently available, it is finally possible to achieve a global perspective on spirituality. And this could not exist apart from the emergence of a global economy and the sense that we all live in *one world* now.

Some Conclusions

So what have we learned about spirituality in this book? I think it makes sense to think of our spiritual life as a journey toward enlightenment and truth. A spiritual life is a meaningful life, it is fulfilling and satisfying, and this is why the most spiritual people are often the most joyful and happy people we know. Some people may desire the spiritual discipline that comes with a life of prayer and service, but spirituality does not have to involve withdrawal from the world and the renunciation of individual joys such as family, friendship, and love. As we have seen, spirituality involves a celebration of the sacred character of this life. On the other hand, spirituality takes a distance from purely material things, including wealth, success, and power, and it overcomes the sense of the self as a completely separate ego. In this book, I have emphasized that spirituality requires attention to *this* life: How should I live? How can I be more completely attuned or engaged with the world? What really matters when all is said and done? And I have tried to make sense of spiritual life by focusing on the most important aspects of spirituality or the four steps on the path of enlightenment. These include:

1. Staying open to suffering, whether this is your own or somebody else's. This means not hardening yourself, but showing compassion which is the only authentic response to suffering;

2. Living a generous life, or *becoming* the generosity of the world, in the sense of giving the best of yourself to others, through caring, forgiveness, and love.

3. Cultivating mindfulness and wonder, which returns one to the magical quality of the world, and the experience of the sacred, which is absolutely present in this moment, now.

4. Accepting death but returning to joy as the proper attitude towards life and death. This means accepting that our lives are a part of nature, but in spite of our mortality we must remain open for happiness and joy.

All of this suggests four different dimensions of spiritual experience, focused respectively on the self, the other, life, and death. Along the way, I have discussed various spiritual practices that could enhance each of these aspects of our lives, including meditation, prayer, thought experiments, and parables, as well as stories and arguments that can orient us toward spiritual fulfillment.

But spirituality is a very complex field. And there are many spiritual themes and practices. Why should we think that precisely *these* four steps are the most essential aspects of spiritual life? This is an important question, and in response, I want to argue that while there are other aspects of spirituality that must be taken seriously, these four steps affirm the basic goodness of the world, and nothing else can be the key to spiritual life. This certainly does not mean that everything that happens is good. We rejected that idea in the first chapter. What it does mean is this:

1. Everyone and everything is interconnected and interdependent. And in compassion I can affirm this because the suffering and well-being of others is something that matters to me: it enlarges my sense of who I am, while my own suffering returns me to the real world. In this sense, life is one.

2. Life is a principle of absolute generosity and abundance. And in generous actions like forgiveness I can affirm this by sacrificing something—my possessions, my time, my own spiritual comfort, or my life—for the sake of others. In this way, living a generous life reflects the ultimate generosity of life itself.

3. The world is a sacred place, full of miracles and marvels. And in mindfulness and wonder I can affirm this by leaving the narrow confines of my own life to experience the deeper realities of existence itself. This means that even with the rise of *information*, the world is still a mysterious, miraculous place, and it is sacred.

4. Life is inherently meaningful. And in coming to terms with death, I am able to affirm this when I experience the meaning of life as something that is given to me here and now, in the context of my own mortality. But mortality is not a gloomy truth that we must yield to, and joy remains a possibility that we can return to since the world is full of meaning.

More than anything else, then, spirituality involves having *trust* in the basic goodness of life, and this is to affirm that life is one. It is generous. It is sacred. And it is inherently meaningful, even if our own existence is transitory.

Spiritual Skill

The spiritual journey is never a straightforward movement from one point to another. There will always be setbacks and distractions, and sometimes this can mean two steps forward and one step back; but we can make progress if we focus on spiritual themes and affirm the cultivation of spiritual life as an explicit intention that we must set for ourselves. We cannot expect to have a spiritual experience whenever we want to, but we can remain open to spiritual experiences. And we can become more open and attuned to spirituality through the continual practice of meditation, prayer, and other spiritual forms, including philosophy.

In the classic Daoist philosophical work called *The Book of Chuang Tzu*, there are several stories about craftsmen—cooks and wheelwrights, fishermen, and woodcarvers—who have become completely skilled or proficient in their craft. In each case, the stories suggest a kind of analogy between the perfection of manual artistry and "living according to the Dao," which is just another way of talking about the most complete attunement to life itself. For example, Woodcarver Ching carves a piece of wood to use as a bell support. But everyone who sees it is astonished because it looks as if "ghosts or spirits had done it." It really is that good! The Marquis of Lu is amazed, and asks Woodcarver Ching, "Where does your art come from?"

> "I am just a woodcarver," Ching replied. "How could I have 'art'? One thing is certain, though, that when I carve a bell support, I do not allow it to exhaust my original breath, so I take care to calm my heart. After I have fasted for three days, I give no thought to praise, reward, titles or income. After I have fasted for five days, I give no thought to glory or blame, to skill or stupidity. After I have fasted for seven days, I am so still that I forget whether I have four limbs and a body. By then the Duke and his court have ceased to exist as far as I am concerned. All my energy is focused and external concerns are gone. After that I depart and enter the mountain forest, and explore the Heavenly innate nature of the trees; once I find one with a perfect shape, I can see for certain the possibility of a bell support and I set my hand to the task; if I cannot see the possibility, I leave it be. By doing so, I harmonize the Heavenly with Heaven, and perhaps this is why it is thought that my carvings are done by spirits!"[1]

Now this is an extravagant story, and we are meant to be impressed by Ching's devotion to his craft, his facility with wood, and his complete understanding of its basic nature. On the one hand, the story suggests that by cultivating our own skill or craft—whether this is woodworking, music, teaching, or anything else—we can become more spiritually centered and accomplished in the rest of our lives. But it also implies the possibility of spiritual fulfillment in harmonizing one's own "Heavenly" nature with "Heaven" itself. This is done by clearing the mind of all distractions, focusing on the challenge at hand, and living a spiritual life with dedication and

1. The story of woodcarver Ching appears in *The Book of Chuang Tzu*, 162–63.

extreme devotion but without regard to selfish goals or outcomes—focussing on the work but not on the rewards of work. In this story, it's all about living according to the *Dao,* which means the most complete attunement to *this* life, which requires wisdom, self-understanding, and a learned spontaneity that comes from much experience and practice. So in everything we do, we should try to be like Woodcarver Ching; and in this way we will eventually become skilled practitioners of our own (spiritual) craft.

Woodcarver Ching doesn't consider himself to be an artist. He seems to think of himself as a humble carpenter, and he has no pretensions to being anything more than this. I think the point here is that most ordinary activities—like cooking, cleaning, or woodcarving—can also be practiced in a spiritual way; everyday life and spiritual life are not mutually exclusive; and the only way to achieve proficiency in *anything*—including spirituality—comes through continual practice, which leads to self-overcoming. If the goal of spiritual life is enlightenment, then this involves being spiritually proficient, and skillful, in the same sort of way that Ching is proficient as a woodcarver. As spiritual practitioners, we are continually preparing ourselves through mindfulness, spiritual exercises, and experience so that eventually we know exactly what to do even in the most challenging circumstances. And sometimes we won't even have to think about it, because it has become a part of who we are.

The spirituality of life is important even though it is something that we frequently ignore. And enlightenment is something that we can strive for. But what is the final goal of enlightenment? Is enlightenment like a religious conversion, where the moment of insight involves a complete reorientation of our being? Or is it a matter of continual enhancement towards God or the Good or whatever the highest principle is held to be? I think that enlightenment can be found in both possibilities. Sometimes people undergo experiences that abruptly change their ordinary attitudes and responses to the world: An illness, a near-death experience, or the death of someone you love may force you to reexamine how you live your life, and this could lead to an abrupt spiritual change. Most of the time, however, spirituality is an ongoing part of our life that continually challenges and inspires us. It enhances our life while at the same time it can makes us uneasy with some of the choices that we have made for ourselves; and so we resolve to change things. And in the long run, we are bound to make progress, if spirituality becomes an explicit priority for us, and we are prepared to do some spiritual work. Spiritual rewards are usually in proportion to the effort that we put into our spiritual lives; and *if we want it, we will find it*—for instance, we find the teacher who seems to enter our life just when we feel that we need one. So we should not be dismayed; and the truth will meet us halfway if that is really what we want!

The whole idea of enlightenment simply means that something—in this case our spiritual life—has become more clearly defined, and that much easier to experience or make sense of. And in this regard, the four steps on the path of enlightenment can help to clarify the nature of spirituality and its most important themes. Once again, these are the spiritual rules that underlie this insight:

1. Stay open to suffering

2. Live a generous life

3. Cultivate mindfulness and wonder

4. Accept death and return to joy

These four steps on the path of enlightenment are the most basic aspects of spiritual truth. And by embracing them, we can affirm our spiritual life, which is given to us *here* and *now*.

Our spiritual life is vast, like the physical world around us; but we know so little about it. We have only begun to explore the spiritual world that we belong to, and for the most part it remains an unknown territory. But there are some basic ideas that can help us on our way, and in this book I have tried to describe them. The great spiritual traditions—both religious and philosophical—can help us to understand our everyday experience and our sense of attunement to this world. And through reflection on these things—and the four steps on the path of enlightenment—we can start to live in a more spiritually accomplished way.

Bibliography

Améry, Jean. *At the Mind's Limits: Contemplations by a Survivor on Auschwitz and Its Realities.* Translated by Sidney Rosenfeld and Stella P. Rosenfeld. Bloomington: Indiana University Press, 1980.

Aristotle. *Nicomachean Ethics.* In *The Basic Works of Aristotle.* Edited by Richard McKeon. New York: Random House, 1941.

Bacon, Ed. *8 Habits of Love.* New York: Grand Central Life and Style, 2012.

Black Elk. *Black Elk Speaks, Being the Life Story of a Holy Man, as told to John G. Neihardt.* Lincoln: University of Nebraska Press, 1988.

Cantacuzino, Marina. *The Forgiveness Project: Stories for a Vengeful Age.* Philadelphia: Kingsley, 2016.

Chödrön, Pema. *The Places that Scare You.* Boston: Shambhala, 2001.

Chuang Tzu. *The Book of Chuang Tzu.* Translated by Martin Palmer. London: Penguin/Arkana, 1996.

Connor, Kelly. *To Cause a Death.* Forest Row, UK: Clairview, 2004.

Conze, Edward, ed. *Buddhist Scriptures.* Harmondsworth, UK: Penguin, 1983.

Dalai Lama. *The Art of Happiness: A Handbook for Living.* New York: Riverhead, 1998.

———. *Ethics for the New Millennium.* New York: Riverhead, 1999.

———. *How to Expand Love.* New York: Atria, 2005.

Danto, Arthur. *The Transfiguration of the Commonplace.* Cambridge: Harvard University Press, 1983.

Derrida, Jacques. "On Forgiveness." In *On Cosmopolitanism and Forgiveness*, 25–60. Translated by Mark Dooley and Michael. Hughes. London: Routledge, 2002.

Epictetus. *The Handbook.* Translated by Nicholas White. HPC Philosophical Classics Series. Indianapolis: Hackett, 1983.

Epicurus. "Letter to Menoeceus." In *The Stoic and Epicurean Philosophers*, edited by Whitney Oates, 30–33. New York: Random House, 1940.

Hadot, Pierre. *Philosophy as a Way of Life: Spiritual Exercises from Socrates to Foucault.* Translated by Michael Chase. Oxford: Blackwell, 1995.

Holy Bible: Revised Standard Version. New York: Collins, 1973.

Ilibagiza, Immaculee. *Left to Tell: Discovering God amidst the Rwandan Holocaust.* Carlsbad, CA: Hay House, 2006.

Jung, Carl. *Memories, Dreams, Reflections.* Edited by Aniela Jaffé. Translated by Richard and Clara Winston. New York: Random House, 1973.

Kandinsky, Wassily. "Reminiscences." In *Modern Artists on Art*, edited by Robert L. Herbert, 19–39. 2nd ed. Mineola, NY: Dover, 2000.

———. *Concerning the Spiritual in Art*. Translated by M. Sadler. Boston: MFA Publications, 2006.

Kaufmann, Moisés. *The Laramie Project*. New York: Vintage, 2001.

Loori, John. *Riding the Ox Home: Stages on the Path of Enlightenment*. Boston: Shambhala, 2002.

Lucretius. *On the Nature of the Universe*. Translated by R. E. Latham. Penguin Classics. London: Penguin, 1994.

Marcus Aurelius. *Meditations*. Translated by M. Staniforth. Penguin Classics. Harmondsworth, UK: Penguin, 1964.

The Matthew Shepard Foundation. Website. "Mission." http://www.matthewshepard.org/about-us.

McCreary, Alf. *Gordon Wilson: An Ordinary Hero*. London: Pickering, 1996.

Montaigne, Michel de. *The Complete Essays of Montaigne*. Translated by Donald Frame. Stanford: Stanford University Press, 2002.

Nietzsche, Friedrich. *The Gay Science*. Translated by Walter Kaufmann. New York: Vintage, 1974.

———. *The Twilight of the Idols*. In *The Portable Nietzsche*, edited by Walter Kaufmann, 463–564. London: Chatto & Windus, 1971.

Nussbaum, Martha. *Upheavals of Thought: The Intelligence of Emotions*. Cambridge: Cambridge University Press, 2003.

Pietsch, William. *The Serenity Prayer Book*. New York: Harper, 1992.

Plato. *Apology*. Translated by Benjamin Jowett. In *Plato: Six Great Dialogues*. Mineola, NY: Dover, 2007.

———. *Phaedo*. Translated by Benjamin Jowett. In *Plato: Six Great Dialogues*. Mineola, NY: Dover, 2007.

———. *Republic*. Translated by Benjamin Jowett. In *The Dialogues of Plato: Volume 4*. London: Sphere, 1970.

———. *Symposium*. Translated by Michael Joyce. In *The Collected Dialogues of Plato, including the Letters*, edited by Edith Hamilton and Huntington Cairns. Bollingen Series 71. Princeton: Princeton University Press, 1978.

Reps, Paul, and Nyogen Senzaki, comps. *Zen Flesh, Zen Bones: A Collection of Zen and Pre-Zen Writings*. Boston: Tuttle, 1998.

Rilke, Rainer Maria. *Duino Elegies*. Translated by Edward Snow. New York: North Point, 2001.

Rousseau, Jean-Jacques. *Reveries of the Solitary Walker*. Translated by Peter France. Penguin Classics. Harmondsworth, UK: Penguin, 1979.

Rumi, *The Mathnawi of Jalalu'ddin Rumi*. Vol. 3. Translated by Reynold Nicholson. London: Luzac, 1977.

Scheffler, Samuel. *Death and the Afterlife*. Edited by Nico Kolodny. Berkeley Tanner Lectures. Oxford: Oxford University Press, 2013.

Shah, Idris. *Tales of the Dervishes*, 155–57. New York: Penguin-Arkana, 1993.

Shelley, Percy Bysshe. "A Defence of Poetry." In *The Great Critics*, edited by James Smith and Edd Parks, 553–83. New York: Norton, 1960.

———. "Epipsychidion." In *Shelley: Poetical Works*, edited by Thomas Hutchinson, 411–30. Oxford: Oxford University Press, 1970.

BIBLIOGRAPHY

Tolstoy, Leo. *The Death of Ivan Ilych*. Translated by Aylmer Maude. In *The Death of Ivan Ilych, and Other Stories*, 95–156. Signet Classic. New York: New American Library, 1960.

Easwaran, Eknath, trans. *The Upanishads*. Petaluma, CA: Nilgiri, 1987.

Wiesenthal, Simon. *The Sunflower: On the Possibilities and Limits of Forgiveness*. Rev. and exp. ed. 2nd paperback ed. New York: Schocken, 1998.

Index

Index